BETTING THE KENTUCKY DERBY

Acknowledgments

*T*HERE'S NO DISPUTING the fact that the Kentucky Derby is one of the most convoluted races to handicap, and one of the toughest to bet with confidence. There are so many variables that can control the outcome of the race when a full field of immature 3-year-olds congregates side by side in the starting gate. For many entrants the race is won or lost in the paddock several minutes before post time. The pressure and anxiety caused by a robust and enthusiastic crowd of more than 100,000 can weaken the nerves and concentration of the sternest man and beast alike. A likely field of 20 almost ensures a wide trip or blocked journey for several competitors.

Despite all the handicapping adversity, the good news is there's a large rainbow with a pot of gold waiting at the finish line for the well-versed and patient Derby bettor. The opportunity for a lifetime wagering score exists on the Derby itself, the Oaks the day before, and the lucrative betting cards surrounding each big event. The pools are gigantic, much of the betting public is uninformed, and the wagering opportunities are limitless. The rewards are well worth the risks. My goal in producing this handbook was to make you, the bettor, more knowledgeable and better equipped to confidently wager on America's greatest horse race. I believe we've succeeded in doing just that. I hope you agree and enjoy the ride.

I'd like to give a special thanks to Steven Crist and Robin Foster for their unmatched editing skills and never-ending enthusiasm for Thoroughbred racing, which helped to make this handbook all that much better. Thanks also to Brent Diamond and Jim Kostas for allowing me to contribute a second book to the DRF *Elements of Handicapping* series. Thanks to my other external racing contacts and *Daily Racing Form* co-workers, friends, and colleagues for their contributions and their support of this project: Mike Beer, Andrew Beyer, Duane Burke, Maria Cavalari, Mark Cramer, Chris Donofry, Jim Fasolino, Sarah Feldman, Brad Free, Lonnie Goldfeder, Lila Kerns, Addis O'Connell, Steve Marcinak, Mandy Minger, Tim O'Leary, Chris Stango, Adrianne Tovar, Melissa Ullmann, and Mike Watchmaker. And, finally, to my wife Lou-Ann, a universe of gratitude for her love, patience, and support. Thanks for agreeing to trade the new kitchen-appliance money for a January Derby future bet on Fusaichi Pegasus. It makes filling the ice trays that much more bearable.

Contents

BETTING THE KENTUCKY DERBY

1

BIG-RACE DAYS

WHEN I WAS 11 or 12 years old I used to enthusiastically walk a mile or so from my parents' rental up Central Avenue to Yonkers Raceway, now known as the illustrious Empire City Racino. Back in those days I was financially loaded for bear. My bankroll consisted of $5, and I would like to say I earned it by mowing the neighbor's lawn or taking out the trash. The truth is, my father gave me the $5 starting bankroll. Now that I look back many years later, it probably was some type of small-time bribe for all the afternoons we snuck off to the track when my mother thought we were at the beach, zoo, amusement park, shopping for groceries, or at a Yankees game. I believe the correct term for my old man was "juvenile enabler."

My father was even kind enough to throw in an advance program, which he picked up at Dan's Tobacco & Candy store after working the 12:00 to 8:00 shift. In those days, $5 was all a responsible and patient harness handicapper needed to succeed. If you could expertly and confidently collect 9 or 10 show bets on drivers Carmine Abbatiello and Rejean Daigneault at $2.60 or $2.80 a pop, you were well on your way to a successful career. On the good nights when Carmine or Rejean didn't make an unexpected stretch break at 3–5, I'd leave the track with a $12 or $15 profit. All was well in the world of high-stakes harness-racing betting.

Unfortunately, a lot has changed since the days of my harness-racing show parlays. The game has gotten considerably tougher to beat with a traditional "grind-along" style of play while attempting to compete with shrewder players and unimaginable advancements in technology. For starters, the parimutuel competition is much more prepared today than it was 15 or 20 years ago. Intricate computer programs that can track live odds and weaknesses in the betting pools, advanced trainer and pedigree information, superior speed and pace figures, and sophisticated betting syndicates (which are heavily bankrolled and professionally managed) in the United States and overseas make it much more difficult for the average player to find any value.

Today, there are only a handful of bettors that consistently wager on the traditional win, place, and show format with any degree of success. There are just too many obstacles for this type of player to succeed in today's game. But do not despair! Today's horseplayer has a tremendous opportunity that was not available to his counterpart of several decades ago—a vast array of betting options beyond win, place, and show.

That's a strong advantage in day-to-day play, but even more so on racing's biggest days—and there is no bigger day or bigger opportunity than America's most famous horse race, the Kentucky Derby at Churchill Downs on the first Saturday in May.

BIG-RACE-DAY GUARANTEED MULTI-RACE POOLS

TODAY, THE MOST successful players are those that consistently adjust to the changing times and have learned to save their bankrolls for the bettor-friendly, multi-race bets, many of which have guaranteed pools.

In these types of pools we're essentially looking for a collection of bettors that consist of the fewest tiger sharks and are instead bloated with schools of lazy winter flounder. Where do we find these uninformed, lethargic bettors? Fortunately, they exist almost every weekend of the year at racetracks across the country. The following monthly schedule of racetracks and big-race days offers the savvy handicapper the opportunity to play into portly pools where there are guaranteed to be uninformed bettors coughing up uninformed dollars.

These types of days are what I like to call the New Year's Eve of racing days. You have your amateur sloppy drinkers on New Year's Eve, and you have your legion of recreational bettors on big-race days. There's nothing more appealing to the seasoned pro than watching the "Uncle Leos" and "Cousin Gracies" of the world betting on birthdays, anniversaries, favorite colors, and names of horses and jockeys. These big-race days are usually heavily advertised in the local media and consistently bring out novice fans and fledgling bettors. Mark your calendars and clear out the bank account.

Month	Racetrack	Big-Race Days
January	Gulfstream/Santa Anita	Sunshine Millions
February	Gulfstream Park	Swale, Holy Bull Stakes, Donn Handicap
February	Fair Grounds	Mineshaft H., Fair Grounds Handicap, Silverbulletday Stakes, Risen Star Stakes
March	Gulfstream Park	Gulfstream Park Handicap, Hutcheson Stakes, Richter Scale Handicap, Fountain of Youth
March	Santa Anita	Frank E. Kilroe Mile Handicap, Robert B. Lewis Stakes, Santa Anita Handicap
March	Aqueduct	Gotham Stakes
March	Fair Grounds	Fair Grounds Oaks, Louisiana Derby
March	Bay Meadows	El Camino Real Derby
March	Santa Anita	Santa Anita Oaks
March	Tampa Bay Downs	Hillsborough Stakes, Tampa Bay Derby
March	Sunland Park	WinStar Oaks, WinStar Derby
March	Turfway Park	Lane's End Stakes
March	Nad Al Sheba (Dubai)	Dubai World Cup, UAE Derby
March	Gulfstream Park	Florida Derby
April	Aqueduct	Bay Shore Stakes, Wood Memorial

Month	Racetrack	Big-Race Days
April	Santa Anita	Santa Anita Derby, Potrero Grande Handicap
April	Hawthorne	Illinois Derby
April	Aqueduct	Carter Handicap, Withers Stakes
April	Keeneland	Vinery Madison Stakes, Stonerside Beaumont Stakes, Maker's Mark Mile, Toyota Blue Grass Stakes, Commonwealth Stakes, Coolmore Lexington Stakes
April	Oaklawn Park	Arkansas Derby
May	Churchill Downs	Kentucky Oaks, Kentucky Derby
May	Lone Star Park	Lone Star Derby
May	Pimlico	Black-Eyed Susan, Preakness
May	Belmont Park	Peter Pan, Metropolitan Handicap
May	Hollywood Park	Shoemaker Mile Stakes, Gamely Stakes
June	Thistledown	Ohio Derby
June	Belmont Park	Belmont Stakes, Mother Goose Stakes, Suburban Handicap
June	Colonial Downs	All Along Stakes, Colonial Turf Cup
June	Churchill Downs	Stephen Foster Handicap
June	Prairie Meadows	Iowa Oaks
June	Hollywood Park	Hollywood Gold Cup
July	Hastings	Lt. Governor's Handicap
July	Woodbine	King Edward Stakes
July	Belmont Park	Dwyer Stakes
July	Calder	Princess Rooney Handicap, Smile Sprint Handicap, Carry Back Stakes
July	Monmouth Park	United Nations
July	Hollywood Park	American Oaks, Triple Bend Handicap, CashCall Mile, Swaps Stakes
July	Delaware Park	Delaware Oaks
July	Colonial Downs	Virginia Derby

Month	Racetrack	Big-Race Days
July	Del Mar	Eddie Read Handicap, Bing Crosby Handicap
July	Saratoga	Whitney Handicap, Go For Wand, Alfred G. Vanderbilt Handicap, Diana Handicap, Jim Dandy
August	Saratoga	Alabama, King's Bishop, Travers, Sword Dancer Invitational
August	Del Mar	Del Mar Handicap, Pacific Classic
August	Mountaineer Park	West Virginia Derby
August	Monmouth Park	Oceanport Stakes, Matchmaker Stakes, Haskell Invitational
August	Arlington Park	Secretariat Stakes, Arlington Million, Beverly D. Stakes
September	Saratoga	Woodward, Forego Handicap, Spinaway Stakes, Hopeful Stakes
September	Philadelphia Park	Pennsylvania Derby
September	Del Mar	Del Mar Futurity, Del Mar Debutante Stakes
September	Belmont Park	Man o' War, Ruffian Handicap, Futurity Stakes, Gazelle Stakes, Brooklyn Handicap, Jockey Club Gold Cup, Beldame Stakes, Joe Hirsch Turf Classic, Vosburgh Stakes, Flower Bowl Invitational, Kelso Handicap
September	Santa Anita	Yellow Ribbon Stakes, Oak Leaf Stakes, Goodwood Handicap, Norfolk Stakes
September	Woodbine	Woodbine Mile, Canadian Stakes, Summer Stakes
September	Louisiana Downs	Super Derby
September	Turfway Park	Kentucky Cup Classic, Kentucky Cup Juvenile Stakes, Kentucky Cup Sprint, Turfway Stakes
September	Hawthorne	Hawthorne Gold Cup

Month	Racetrack	Big-Race Days
October	Keeneland	Darley Alcibiades Stakes, Sycamore Stakes, Shadwell Turf Mile, Lane's End Breeders' Futurity, Juddmonte Spinster Stakes, Queen Elizabeth II Challenge Cup
October	Belmont Park	Frizette Stakes, Jamaica Handicap, Champagne Stakes, Jerome Handicap
October	Santa Anita	Clement L. Hirsch Turf, Ancient Title Handicap, Lady's Secret Handicap, Oak Tree Mile
October	Woodbine	Canadian International, E.P. Taylor Stakes
October	Breeders' Cup	
November	Aqueduct	Cigar Mile, Remsen Stakes, Discovery Handicap
December	Calder	My Charmer Handicap, Tropical Turf Handicap
December	Hollywood Park	Hollywood Starlet, CashCall Futurity

Every year, around the start of the Triple Crown season and before the Breeders' Cup, acclaimed author and handicapper James Quinn writes an article about the necessity of having a fat wallet in preparation for a realistic assault on these upcoming big-race days. After all, these are the days when potential boxcar exotic scores exist and there are plenty of ripe apples in the betting basket. This sound money-management advice is one that the average handicapper and player should adhere to. In fact, I'd even go so far as to recommend that you cut out Quinn's annual betting-advice column and give it a permanent space on the refrigerator next to the household-chore wish list that's collecting dust. Although each handicapper's betting platform and financial comfort zone differs, do what you can to fatten your bankroll for these types of big-race days—even if it means sitting on the betting sidelines for several weeks.

Remember: It only takes a few races and one special afternoon to make up for months of missed photos and tough beats.

2

USING BEYER SPEED FIGURES TO EVALUATE DERBY CONTENDERS

*I*T'S SAFE TO SAY there have only been a few handicapping innovations over the last couple of decades that have truly enhanced horseplayers' ability to uncover potential winners. There have probably been hundreds of others that have come and gone after failing miserably because of poor handicapping logic or unstable variables.

One of the most vital developments for handicappers has been the availability of Beyer Speed Figures, which debuted in *The Racing Times* in 1991 and now appear exclusively in *Daily Racing Form*. Andrew Beyer has been the horse-racing columnist for the *Washington Post* since 1978 and has been considered one of the leading experts on Thoroughbred racing and wagering for the last 30 years. He has written four books on racing, the most influential of which was *Picking Winners*. First published in 1975, during an era when a horse's class and conditioning were thought to be the most reliable and helpful handicapping factors, this book altered the practice of speed handicapping and the composition of speed-figure charts for all time.

Beyer did not invent the concept of using speed figures, but when he agreed to publish his figures as part of the past performances in

1991, it was a revolutionary development for horseplayers. Nearly three decades later, they remain one of the most powerful and popular handicapping tools available.

WHAT IS A BEYER SPEED FIGURE?

IF EVERY HORSE ran over a standard surface at the same distance, we could compare their abilities simply by looking at their unadjusted, or "raw," final times, but life is not that simple. Different tracks are faster or slower, and the same track can be fast on a Friday and slow on a Saturday. Speed figures take all these variations into account. Every Thoroughbred in North America is assigned a Beyer Speed Figure after each performance, and they are calibrated to permit comparisons of efforts at different distances. The higher the Beyer Speed Figure, the better the performance. In theory, a horse that earns a Beyer of 101 while running six furlongs at Churchill Downs should be faster than a horse that earns a 92 running one mile at Fair Grounds.

On the Beyer scale of numbers, the premium stakes horses in the country earn figures of 110 or higher. Good allowance horses or low-grade stakes horses run around 100. A typical $25,000 claiming race would be run in the high 80s or low 90s, and a $10,000 claiming race in the high 70s to low 80s. The average winning figure for bottom-level $2,500 claimers at smaller tracks is in the 50s.

Below are the past performances for Curlin, champion 3-year-old and Horse of the Year in 2007. He attained $5.1 million in earnings and won three Grade 1 races, including the Breeders' Cup Classic, and consistently recorded Beyer Speed Figures over 100.

On the other end of the Beyer Speed Figure scale would be the 3-year-old filly Sarahsthejudge. Despite compiling a record of 3 for 7 record at Finger Lakes in 2007, with a combined winning margin of 30½ lengths in decisive scores, she only managed a lifetime-top Beyer Speed Figure of 52 on September 10 and earnings below $20,000. And for a mere $4,000, you could have claimed her and paraded her around the backyard at your 7-year-old daughter's birthday party.

Sarahsthejudge
Own: Dennis Amaty $4,000
Light Blue and Gray Stripes
z G (553 58 65 83 .10) 2007:(557 58 .10)

B. f. 3 (Feb)
Sire: Judge T C (Judge Smells)
Dam: Sarah Rosebud (Unreal Zeal)
Br: Herman Wilensky(NY)
Tr: Rolffs Mikhael (68 7 4 7 .10) 2007:(69 7 .10)

L 117

Life	11	3	0	1	$19,779	52	D.Fst	9	3	0	1	$19,198 52
2007	7	3	0	0	$18,204	52	Wet (325)	2	0	0	0	$581 28
2006	4	M	0	1	$1,575	29	Turf (250)	0	0	0	0	$0 -
FL	7	3	0	0	$18,204	52	Dist (322)	7	3	0	0	$18,204 52

07-1FL gd 170 :234 :48 1:124 1:454 3↑Ⓕ[S]Alw 20600N1R 28 6 46 45 612 711 613¼ Davila M A Jr L120f 5.60 63-24 ScnNHrd1161 ExplsvImpct1203¾ DncngTmbr120no 5w 1/2, tired 8
07-6FL fst 170 :243 :493 1:144 1:46 3↑ⒻClm 7500N3L 52 4 12 11 11 15½ 15¼ Rodriguez P A L118f *1.55 75-21 Sarahsthejudge1185¼ Hopi's Lolo1162 Family Kiss1202¼ Easily 6
07-2FL fst 170 :232 :481 1:14 1:461 3↑ⒻClm 4000N2L 51 2 32½ 21 1hd 12½ 19½ Rodriguez P A L118f *.60 74-28 *Srhsthejudge* 1189½ Strider'sForest1201½ Whlit1163¾ Ridden out 8
07-8FL fst 170 :234 :472 1:121 1:443 3↑ⒻAlw 17600N2L 39 7 89¼ 610 513 512 511 Camejo O L115f 22.50 71-23 *PlesureforMe* 120½ Abbyror1103¾ *AnothrSwti* 1203¼ Lacked rally 9
07-9FL fst 170 :234 :481 1:142 1:462 3↑ⒻMd 4000 48 2 84¼ 74¾ 2½ 14 115¾ Rodriguez P A L119 5.10 73-22 Sarahsthejudge11915 Zip City112nk Petite Plume1246½ Easily 12
07-9FL fst 170 :233 :483 1:151 1:482 3↑ⒻMd 4000 15 5 78½ 63½ 57½ 43½ 47¾ Morales D L119 7.20 55-22 OldHss1193 HhGLhtl1192¼ FrRc1192½ Lacked room 3/16,chkd 9
07-7FL fst 170 :24 :482 1:143 1:48 3↑Ⓕ[S]Md 15000(15-13) 7 4 52 65 713 719 517½ Morales D L118f 8.80 47-25 SumWish1208¾ ShoeFlyPie1181½ GonnGtMrrid1201 Rail, tired 7
eviously trained by Wilensky Herman 2006(as of 12/22): (143 24 24 22 0.17)
06-5Crc fst 1 :232 :48 1:164 1:462 ⒻMd 12500 9 2 48 39 53½ 46 312 Fuentes R D L118b 2.50 47-22 NughtyNeld1182¾ DoubleShow1189¼ Srhsthejudge1183¼ Tired 7
06-1Crc sly5 7f :233 :474 1:142 1:282 ⒻMd 12500 19 4 5 21 32½ 47 410¾ Bridgmohan J V L113b 3.60 60-21 MusclMschf118nk Sowto1189¾ Swtsouthrnfll118¾ Faltered turn 6
06-2Crc fst 7f :23 :473 1:15 1:291 ⒻMd 12500 23 11 5 74¼ 76 76 58 Fuentes M E L118b 6.00 59-22 MissHobi1181½ *MusclMschf* 1181 Mx'sGl1181½ 4 wide, no menace 12
KS: Oct15 FL 3f fst :362 B *2/7* ● Aug21 FL 4f fst :481 H *1/24* Aug7 FL 3f fst :364 H *11/22*
NER: 31-60Days (9 .00 $0.00) Dirt (134 .09 $0.67) Routes (56 .09 $0.57) Claim (94 .10 $0.67) J/T 2006-07 FL (14 .00 $0.00) J/T 2006-07 (14 .00 $0.00)

Is winning at the racetrack as simple as betting the horse with the highest Beyer number? It's a well-known fact that the betting public's choice (favorite) wins approximately 34 percent overall. The percentage of winners with the highest top Beyer figures is not far behind, ranging from 25 to 30 percent regardless of the racetrack or race conditions.

Before you hand in your resignation and cash in the 401(k) for a new career as a professional handicapper, however, you should know that betting blindly on the horse with the highest Beyer Speed Figure in his last or next-to-last race is not the key to uncovering the Yamashita's Gold of horse racing. There are many other variables that affect the outcome of an individual horse race, and these variables must be given the same or equal consideration as Beyer Speed Figures, depending on the circumstances. In addition, most horses with standout Beyer numbers are certain to attract public attention and are often race favorites or second choices.

Once the Beyer Speed Figures first became available to the masses, horses with the highest numbers began to gain the most wagering dollars. In 2008, for example, a horse with the two highest last-race Beyers might be odds-on at 6–5 or 7–5, whereas the same horse in 1982 might have been 2–1 at post time. Therefore, from a parimutuel standpoint, you might reasonably assume that the Beyer Speed Figures have slowly decreased in their effectiveness and value, but that's simply not the case.

Two of the most overlooked top-figure Beyer horses occurred in the last 10 years on Kentucky Derby Day, and both offered tremendous value. The public ignored these 3-year-olds, both of whom produced giant Beyer numbers in their prep races for the big dance. In 1999 it was Charismatic winning at 31–1, and in 2002 War Emblem scored at 20–1.

Charismatic
Own: Lewis Robert B. and Beverly J

Ch. c. 3 (Mar)
Sire: Summer Squall (Storm Bird) $50,000
Dam: Bali Babe (Drone)
Br: Parrish Hill Farm & W. S. Farish (Ky)
Tr: Lukas D. W(0 0 0 0 .00) 2007:(415 49 .12)

Life	17	5	2	4	$2,038,064	108	
1999	10	4	2	1	$2,007,404	108	
1998	7	1	0	3	$30,660	85	
	0	0	0	0	$0	-	
D.Fst	15	5	2	4	$2,035,934		
Wet(314)	1	0	0	0	$2,130		
Synth	0	0	0	0	$0		
Turf(286)	1	0	0	0	$0		
Dst(0)	0	0	0	0	$0		

5Jun99-9Bel	fst	1½	:473 1:12 2:014 2:274	Belmont-G1	107	4	2hd	2½	1hd	2½	31½	Antley C W	L126	*1.60	103-06	LmonDropKid126hd VisionndVrs1261½ Chrismtic1264¾	Drifted, vanned o
15May99-10Pim	fst	1 3/16	:451 1:101 1:351 1:551	Preaknss-G1	107	6	106	107¾	83¾	13	11½	Antley C W	L126	8.40	89-09	Charismatic1261½ Menifee126hd *Badge*1262½	5wd mv,drftd 3/16,drv
1May99-8CD	fst	1¼	:474 1:122 1:372 2:031	KyDerby-G1	108	16	73½	72¾	31½	2½	1nk	Antley C W	L126	31.30	89-14	*Charismatic*126nk Menifee126¾ Cat Thief1261¼	5-wide trip,drivir
18Apr99-8Kee	fst	1 1/16	:231 :464 1:103 1:41	Lexingtn-G2	108	5	65	42½	31½	2hd	12½	Bailey J D	L115	12.10	103-07	*Charismatic*1152½ YnkeeVictor115¾ FindersGold1152	3 wide 2nd turn,drvr
3Apr99-5SA	fst	1⅛	:471 1:112 1:361 1:484	SADerby-G1	94	8	63½	63¾	64	57	48¼	Pincay L Jr	LB120	44.30	83-13	GenrlChllng1203½ PrimTimbr1203½ DsrtHro1201¼	Improved position som
6Mar99-7BM	fst	1 1/16	:224 :46 1:10 1:431	ElCamRlD-G3	95	2	67½	67½	64¾	33½	2hd	Warren R J Jr	LB115	10.60	83-24	Cliquot115hd Charismatic1153½ No Cal Bread117¾	Angled out, rallie
19Feb99-6SA	fst	7f	:214 :434 1:081 1:212	Alw 50000N$Y	94	2	4	59½	59	36½	25	Pincay L Jr	LB117	17.20	93-08	Apremont1195 Charismatic1172 *Forestry*1197	Finished willing
11Feb99-6SA	fst	6½f	:214 :442 1:102 1:171	Clm 62500(62.5-55)	80	8	7	86¼	65	54	2nk	McCarron C J	LB117	2.70	82-17	[D]What Say You110nk Charismatic117nk ValleyDon1171	Bothered near 1,
Placed first through disqualification																	
31Jan99-8SA	gd	1 1/16	:234 :473 1:12 1:424	StCtlina-G2	71	2	52½	54¼	55	57½	513½	Pincay L Jr	LB117	30.10	75-15	GeneralChallenge1173 BuckTrout1201 Brillintly1153½	Bit tight 7/8,wkene
16Jan99-5SA	fst	1 1/16	:233 :472 1:114 1:44	Alw 54000N$Y	78	8	73¼	75¾	73½	73¼	54	Pincay L Jr	LB117	17.90	79-16	Mr. Broad Blade116hd Brilliantly1161 Outstanding Hero1162	Bit tight 3,
27Dec98-1SA	fst	6½f	:213 :441 1:09 1:152	Alw 50000N$Y	85	5	7	78¼	76¾	85¼	34½	Pincay L Jr	LB117	23.10	87-06	*BrightValour*1164 OutstndingHero116½ Chrismtic117nk	Outside,late for 3r
21Nov98-1Hol	fst	6½f	:222 :453 1:104 1:171	Md 62500(62.5-55)	83	3	5	42	41½	12	15	Pincay L Jr	LB119	*1.30	80-20	Charismatic1195 Wandering1192 Pick Up Stixs1196	Rail trip,clearly bes
17Oct98-4SA	fm	1 Ⓣ	:232 :472 1:13 1:381	Md Sp Wt 35k	24	4	11½	11	73¾	812	925¾	McCarron C J	LB120 b	3.40	42-28	LxingtonBch120no DncngMjsty1201¼ *CompnyApprovl*1203½	Speed, stoppe
1Oct98-1SA	fst	1	:221 :452 1:104 1:37	Md Sp Wt 35k	60	2	13	13½	11	22	310¼	Pincay L Jr	LB120 b	2.10	76-15	CrownngStorm12010 NrthrnAvn120nk Chrsmtc1204	Inside, edged for 2n
23Aug98-2Dmr	fst	5½f	:223 :46 :583 1:05	Md Sp Wt 36k	57	2	3	3½	3nk	42½	45	McCarron C J	LB118 b	*.70	83-11	Out in Front1182 Round Four118hd Kona Coast1183	3 wide, weakene
25Jly98-4Dmr	fst	6f	:222 :454 :582 1:112	Md Sp Wt 37k	66	2	6	11	12	2½	31½	Nakatani C S	LB118 b	*2.00	80-12	Prized Demon118½ Seayabyebye1181 Charismatic1186	Inside, outfinishe
20Jun98-3Hol	fst	5f	:222 :453 :574	Md Sp Wt 37k	48	3	4	44¾	35	68½	613¼	Flores D R	B118	12.20	81-15	O'Rey Fantasma1182½ *Aristotle*1182 Buck Trout1183½	Inside, weakene

Conditioned by Hall of Fame trainer D. Wayne Lukas, who had three previous Derby victories to his credit, Charismatic earned a Beyer Speed Figure of 108 less than two weeks before the Derby in the Grade 2 Lexington Stakes at Keeneland. After being dismissed by the betting public, he repeated that number in the Derby, then won the Preakness Stakes and seemed poised to sweep the Triple Crown, but suffered a career-ending injury in the Belmont Stakes.

EIGHTH RACE
Churchill
MAY 1, 1999

1¼ MILES. (1.59^{2}) KENTUCKY DERBY Grade I. Purse $1,000,000 FOR THREE-YEAR-OLDS with an entry fee of $15,000 each and a starting fee of $15,000 each. Supplemental nominations may be made upon payment of $150,000 and in accordance with the rules set forth. All fees, including supplemental nominations, in excess of $500,000 in the aggregate shall be paid to the winner. Churchill Downs Incorporated shall guarantee a minimum gross purse of $1,000,000. The winner shall receive $700,000, second shall receive $170,000, third place shall receive $85,000 and fourth place shall receive $45,000 from the Guaranteed Purse. Colts and Geldings shall each carry a weight of 126 lbs.; Fillies shall each carry 121 lbs.

Value of Race: $1,186,200 Winner $886,200; second $170,000; third $85,000; fourth $45,000. Mutuel Pool $25,849,294.00 Exacta Pool $11,885,521.00 Trifecta Pool $11,240,184.00 Superfecta Pool $1,927,175.00

Last Raced	Horse	M/Eqt.	A.	Wt	PP	¼	½	¾	1	Str	Fin	Jockey	Odds $1
18Apr99 ^{8}Kee^{1}	Charismatic	L	3	126	16	7^{hd}	7^{½}	7^{1½}	3^{1½}	2^{hd}	1^{nk}	Antley C W	31.30
10Apr99 ^{9}Kee^{1}	Menifee	L	3	126	18	14^{1}	17^{1½}	15^{1½}	14^{½}	6^{hd}	2^{¾}	Day P	7.00
10Apr99 ^{9}Kee^{2}	Cat Thief	L b	3	126	10	2^{1½}	2^{1½}	2^{1½}	1^{hd}	1^{½}	3^{1¼}	Smith M E	7.40
3Apr99 ^{5}SA^{2}	Prime Timber	L b	3	126	13	10^{hd}	11^{½}	11^{hd}	5^{½}	4^{hd}	4no	Flores D R	6.30
2Apr99 ^{9}OP^{1}	Excellent Meeting	L	3	121	5	18^{½}	18^{1½}	16^{½}	13^{hd}	9^{hd}	5^{½}	Desormeaux K J	b- 4.80
10Apr99 ^{9}Kee^{4}	Kimberlite Pipe	L	3	126	12	8^{hd}	8^{½}	9^{hd}	7^{hd}	5^{½}	6^{1¼}	Albarado R J	f- 11.60
9Sep98 ^{8}Dmr^{1}	Worldly Manner	L b	3	126	11	3^{hd}	3^{½}	3^{½}	2^{1½}	3^{3½}	7^{½}	Bailey J D	14.50
27Mar99 ^{5}TP^{2}	K One King	L	3	126	9	19	19	18^{1}	16^{½}	13^{1}	8^{1}	Solis A	f- 11.60
10Apr99 ^{9}Kee^{5}	Lemon Drop Kid	L	3	126	19	13^{½}	16^{hd}	17^{1½}	15^{1½}	15^{hd}	9^{nk}	Santos J A	f- 11.60
10Apr99 ^{10}OP^{4}	Answer Lively	L	3	126	7	6^{1½}	5^{hd}	4^{hd}	6^{1½}	7^{1½}	10^{½}	Perret C	37.00
3Apr99 ^{5}SA^{1}	General Challenge	L b	3	126	14	12^{1½}	12^{½}	12^{hd}	10^{hd}	10^{1}	11^{¾}	Stevens G L	b- 4.80
10Apr99 ^{10}OP^{3}	Ecton Park	L b	3	126	3	16^{hd}	15^{hd}	13^{½}	18^{5}	16^{1}	12^{½}	Davis R G	f- 11.60
3Apr99 ^{5}SA^{3}	Desert Hero	L	3	126	6	5^{hd}	6^{½}	6^{hd}	9^{1½}	11^{hd}	13^{1¼}	Nakatani C S	19.70
27Mar99 ^{5}TP^{1}	Stephen Got Even	L	3	126	4	4^{hd}	4^{½}	8^{hd}	12^{hd}	14^{½}	14^{1½}	McCarron C J	5.10
10Apr99 ^{10}OP^{7}	Valhol	L	3	126	8	1^{½}	1^{½}	1^{hd}	4^{½}	12^{1½}	15^{2}	Martinez W	f- 11.60
3Apr99 ^{8}Hia^{1}	First American	L b	3	126	15	15^{hd}	13^{1}	5^{½}	8^{hd}	8^{hd}	16^{2}	Delahoussaye E	34.90
10Apr99 ^{10}Aqu^{1}	Adonis	L b	3	126	1	17^{1½}	14^{hd}	19	17^{1½}	18^{6}	17^{4¾}	Chavez J F	18.70
10Apr99 ^{9}Kee^{3}	Vicar	L f	3	126	17	11^{hd}	9^{hd}	14^{½}	11^{hd}	17^{1½}	18^{3¼}	Sellers S J	8.20
16Mar99 ^{11}GP^{1}	Three Ring	L b	3	121	2	9^{½}	10^{hd}	10^{½}	19	19	19	Velazquez J R	25.60

b-Coupled: Excellent Meeting and General Challenge.
f-Mutuel field: Kimberlite Pipe and K One King and Lemon Drop Kid and Ecton Park and Valhol.

OFF AT 5:29 Start Good For All But. Won . Track fast.
TIME :23^{2}, :47^{4}, 1:12^{2}, 1:37^{2}, 2:03^{1} (:23.52, :47.88, 1:12.52, 1:37.58, 2:03.29)

$2 Mutuel Prices:				
	11 – CHARISMATIC	64.60	27.80	14.40
	13 – MENIFEE		8.40	5.80
	8 – CAT THIEF			5.80

$2 EXACTA 11–13 PAID $727.80 $2 TRIFECTA 11–13–8 PAID $5,866.20
$1 SUPERFECTA 11–13–8–9 PAID $24,015.50

Ch. c, (Mar), by Summer Squall – Bali Babe , by Drone . Trainer Lukas D Wayne. Bred by Parrish Hill Farm & W S Farish (Ky).

Three years later, two-time Derby-winning trainer Bob Baffert, who had scored with Silver Charm in 1997 and Real Quiet in 1998, pulled an upset with a sleek, stunning dark bay colt named War Emblem.

War Emblem
Own: The Thoroughbred Corporation

Dk. b or b. c. 3 (Feb)
Sire: Our Emblem (Mr. Prospector)
Dam: Sweetest Lady (Lord At War*Arg)
Br: Charles Nuckols Jr. & Sons (Ky)
Tr: Baffert Bob(0 0 0 0 .00) 2007:(430 73 .17)

Life	13	7	0	0	$3,491,000	114	D.Fst	12	7	0	0	$3,491,000
2002	10	5	0	0	$3,455,000	114	Wet(344)	0	0	0	0	$0
							Synth	0	0	0	0	$0
2001	3	2	0	0	$36,000	83	Turf(329)	1	0	0	0	$0
	0	0	0	0	$0	-	Dst(0)	0	0	0	0	$0

26Oct02-10AP	fst	1¼		:463 1:101 1:352 2:011	3↑BCClasic-G1	89	3	21½	21	3½	57½	818¼	Espinoza V	L121	4.00	79 -	Volponi1266½ *Medaglia d'Oro*121nk Milwaukee Brew1263	Bid turn, falter
25Aug02-5Dmr	fst	1¼		:452 1:094 1:352 2:012	3↑PacifcCl-G1	110	6	31½	32	2hd	2hd	64¼	Espinoza V	LB117	*1.20	88- 13	CameHome117¾ Momentum1241½ MilwaukeeBrew124½	3wd bid,weaken
4Aug02-11Mth	fst	1⅛		:471 1:103 1:352 1:481	HsklInvH-G1	112	4	1½	1½	11½	14½	13½	Espinoza V	L124	*.30	99- 01	WarEmblem1243½ MagicWeisner118¾ LikeHero1173¾	Bit fractious in ga
8Jun02-10Bel	fst	1½		:48 1:121 2:032 2:293	Belmont-G1	82	9	41½	2hd	52¼	712	819½	Espinoza V	L126	*1.25	64- 12	Sarava126½ *Medaglia d'Oro*1269½ Sunday Break1261	Stumb brk,rank,tir
18May02-12Pim	fst	1 3/16		:46 1:103 1:361 1:561	Preaknes-G1	109	8	2hd	2hd	2hd	11½	1¾	Espinoza V	L126	*2.80	90- 14	WrEmblem126¾ MgicWeisnr126¾ ProudCitizn1261½	Rated 3wd, stiff dri
4May02-9CD	fst	1¼		:47 1:113 1:363 2:01	KyDerby-G1	114	5	11½	11½	11½	11½	14	Espinoza V	L126	20.50	94- 05	*WrEmblem*1264 ProudCitizen126¾ PerfectDrift1263¼	Pace, 3w,hand urgi
Previously trained by Springer Frank R 2002(as of 4/6): (29 8 4 3 0.28)																		
6Apr02-8Spt	fst	1⅛		:481 1:13 1:373 1:494	IllDerby-G2	112	4	11½	11½	12½	15	16¼	Sterling L J Jr	L114	6.30	92- 17	*War Emblem*1146¼ Repent1244½ Fonz's1176½	Ridden o
17Mar02-8Spt	fst	1		:233 :47 1:122 1:391	Alw 48600NC	98	1	11	11½	11½	13	110¾	Juarez A J Jr	L118	*.80	87- 20	*War Emblem*11810¾ *Colorful Tour*1213 Boston Common1158	Drivi
17Feb02-9FG	fst	1 1/16		:23 :46 1:111 1:43	RisenStr-G3	85	3	31	42	41¾	76	69¾	Theriot H J II	L117	38.80	85- 08	*Repent*1222¼ BobsImage1153 Esyfromthegitgo1222¼	Ranged up 3w, fad
26Jan02-9FG	fst	1		:24 :472 1:12 1:374	Lecomte100k	86	3	2hd	1½	1½	2½	52¼	Theriot H J II	L117	12.40	93- 07	Esyfromthgitgo114no SkyTrrc119¾ Itsllinthchs1221¼	Faltered final 1/16
23Nov01-8FG	fst	1		:231 :471 1:122 1:39	Alw 32000N1x	83	6	53¼	3nk	11	13	14½	Theriot H J II	L119	2.00	84- 19	War Emblem1194½ No Trouble1196 Ski Hero1191	Kept to ta
20Oct01-8AP	gd	1	Ⓣ	:233 :474 1:123 1:393	Manila75k	44	10	21	1hd	2hd	75¾	717½	Juarez A J Jr	116	8.00	65- 20	Rylstone1163 U S S Tinosa1201½ Jaha1164	Tired, bl
4Oct01-5AP	fst	1		:23 :454 1:111 1:391	Md Sp Wt 28k	69	1	1hd	11	1½	14	11¾	Juarez A J Jr	121	16.40	78- 23	War Emblem1211¾ Castner1212 Thrym1211½	Drivi

Baffert had taken over the training duties of War Emblem from little-known Midwest conditioner Frank "Bobby" Springer less than a month before the Derby. After War Emblem earned a staggering wire-to-wire victory and 112 Beyer in the Illinois Derby, the colt had been purchased by Prince Ahmed bin Salman and turned over to Baffert. Widely dismissed as a one-dimensional speedball, War Emblem put on an almost identical wire-to-wire uncontested performance at Churchill Downs and posted a 114 Beyer. Who says there's no value in betting the top Beyer Speed Figure in the Kentucky Derby?

NINTH RACE
Churchill
MAY 4, 2002

$1\frac{1}{4}$ MILES. (1.59^{2}) KENTUCKY DERBY Grade I. Purse \$1,000,000 (plus \$1,000,000 Racing Series Bonus) FOR THREE-YEAR-OLDS with an entry fee of \$15,000 each and a starting fee of \$15,000 each. Supplemental nominations may be made upon payment of \$150,000 and in accordance with the rules set forth. Churchill Downs Incorporated shall guarantee a minimum gross purse of \$1,000,000. The winner shall receive \$700,000, second place shall receive \$170,000, third place shall receive \$85,000 and fourth place shall receive \$45,000 from the Guaranteed Purse. Starters shall be named through the entry box on Wednesday, May 1, 2002 at 10:00 a.m. Eastern Daylight Time. Colts and Geldings shall each carry a weight of 126 lbs; Fillies shall each carry 121 lbs.

alue of Race: \$2,175,000 Winner \$1,875,000; second \$170,000; third \$85,000; fourth \$45,000. Mutuel Pool \$34,083,706.00 Exacta Pool 6,069,772.00 Trifecta Pool \$16,910,173.00 Superfecta Pool \$3,965,135.00

ast Raced	Horse	M/Eqt.	A.	Wt	PP	¼	½	¾	1	Str	Fin	Jockey	Odds \$1
Apr02 ^{8}Spt^{1}	War Emblem	L	3	126	5	$1^{\frac12}$	$1^{1\frac12}$	$1^{1\frac12}$	$1^{1\frac12}$	$1^{1\frac12}$	1^{4}	Espinoza V	20.50
Apr02 ^{8}Kee^{1}	Proud Citizen	L	3	126	12	2^{1}	$2^{\frac12}$	$2^{\frac12}$	3^{1}	2^{hd}	$2^{\frac34}$	Smith M E	23.30
3Mar02 ^{10}TP^{1}	Perfect Drift	L	3	126	3	4^{hd}	3^{1}	$3^{\frac12}$	2^{hd}	$3^{3\frac12}$	$3^{3\frac14}$	Delahoussaye E	7.90
3Apr02 ^{8}Aqu^{2}	Medaglia d'Oro	L	3	126	9	10^{1}	9^{1}	$7^{\frac12}$	8^{3}	6^{1}	$4^{1\frac12}$	Pincay L Jr	6.90
3Mar02 ^{10}TP^{3}	Request for Parole	L	3	126	7	6^{hd}	$5^{\frac12}$	5^{hd}	5^{hd}	$5^{\frac12}$	$5^{\frac34}$	Albarado R J	29.80
Apr02 ^{5}SA^{1}	Came Home	L	3	126	14	$3^{\frac12}$	$4^{\frac12}$	$4^{\frac12}$	4^{2}	$4^{\frac12}$	6^{2}	McCarron C J	8.20
3Apr02 ^{9}Kee^{1}	Harlan's Holiday	L	3	126	13	$9^{\frac12}$	$11^{1\frac12}$	8^{hd}	6^{hd}	7^{1}	$7^{\frac34}$	Prado E S	6.00
Apr02 ^{8}Cur^{2}	Johannesburg	L	3	126	1	$11^{\frac12}$	10^{1}	$10^{\frac12}$	$9^{\frac12}$	8^{1}	8no	Stevens G L	8.10
3Mar02 ^{3}NAS^{1}	Essence of Dubai	L b	3	126	8	13^{2}	12^{hd}	12^{hd}	$7^{\frac12}$	9^{3}	9^{1}	Flores D R	10.00
3Apr02 ^{8}Aqu^{4}	Saarland	L	3	126	15	17^{2}	17^{2}	$14^{\frac12}$	16^{hd}	$13^{\frac12}$	$10^{2\frac12}$	Velazquez J R	6.90
3Apr02 ^{8}Aqu^{5}	Blue Burner	L b	3	126	18	5^{hd}	$8^{\frac12}$	$9^{1\frac12}$	$10^{\frac12}$	11^{hd}	$11^{\frac12}$	Day P	24.20
Apr02 LIN^{1}	Castle Gandolfo	L	3	126	11	15^{hd}	15^{1}	$15^{\frac12}$	14^{1}	$12^{2\frac12}$	$12^{4\frac14}$	Bailey J D	14.50
Apr02 ^{5}SA^{2}	Easy Grades	L	3	126	17	12^{1}	14^{hd}	16^{hd}	11^{hd}	14^{2}	13^{nk}	Chavez J F	43.80
3Apr02 ^{11}OP^{1}	Private Emblem	L	3	126	10	7^{1}	7^{hd}	$11^{1\frac12}$	12^{hd}	10^{1}	$14^{4\frac12}$	Meche D J	22.40
Apr02 ^{5}SA^{3}	Lusty Latin	L b	3	126	4	18	18	18	18	18	$15^{2\frac14}$	Corbett G W	22.10
3Apr02 ^{11}OP^{9}	It'sallinthechase	L	3	126	16	$16^{2\frac12}$	16^{hd}	17^{2}	$13^{1\frac12}$	15^{3}	$16^{2\frac34}$	Martin E M Jr	94.50
3Apr02 ^{9}Kee^{3}	Ocean Sound-Ire	L	3	126	6	14^{hd}	$13^{1\frac12}$	13^{1}	17^{2}	17^{2}	$17^{2\frac14}$	Solis A	48.70
3Apr02 ^{11}OP^{2}	Wild Horses	L	3	126	2	$8^{\frac12}$	6^{1}	6^{hd}	15^{hd}	$16^{\frac12}$	18	Douglas R R	58.50

OFF AT 6:12 Start Good. Won driving. Track fast.

TIME :23^{1}, :47, 1:11^{3}, 1:36^{3}, 2:01 (:23.25, :47.04, 1:11.75, 1:36.70, 2:01.13)

\$2 Mutuel Prices:				
	5 – WAR EMBLEM	**43.00**	**22.80**	**13.60**
	13 – PROUD CITIZEN		**24.60**	**13.40**
	3 – PERFECT DRIFT			**6.40**

\$2 EXACTA 5–13 PAID \$1,300.80 \$2 TRIFECTA 5–13–3 PAID \$18,373.20
\$1 SUPERFECTA 5–13–3–9 PAID \$91,764.50

Dk. b or br. c, (Feb), by Our Emblem – Sweetest Lady , by Lord At War-Arg . Trainer Baffert Bob. Bred by Charles uckols Jr & Sons (Ky).

Despite their popularity and widespread use, Beyer Speed Figures are still one of the most powerful handicapping instruments available and continue to offer betting value when applied appropriately. Modern speed handicappers who have managed to incorporate other important handicapping variables into their routine, and have learned to effectively interpret these numbers, still hold a comfortable edge over rival bettors who are not as well-versed.

As Beyer himself suggested in Joe Cardello's *Speed to Spare: Beyer Speed Figures Uncovered* (DRF Press, 2003), "To profit from figures today, a horseplayer may have to look harder for the right spots, and to use figures with some ingenuity, but money-making opportunities are still abundant." Fortunately, on Kentucky Oaks and Kentucky Derby Day there are plenty of casual and uninformed bettors swelling the pools, and, as Beyer suggests, plenty of lucrative wagering opportunities.

No matter what other methods you might incorporate in your race analysis, evaluating contenders by using Beyer Speed Figures is the most logical place to begin the process. If you traditionally use these figures as a part of your handicapping regimen, the same type of game plan should be applied for the Kentucky Derby and on Oaks Day. The key to utilizing them most effectively is finding circumstances where they offer the most value. You might be able to uncover a horse that had a legitimate excuse for running an inferior figure in his last or next-to-last recent effort. The track might have been sloppy. He could have been hindered by an awful inside or outside post position, or maybe he was a victim of a horrendously wide trip. You may find that based on some of his efforts three or four races back, this same horse is more than competitive against today's rivals with a simple return to his best Beyer Speed Figure.

BEYER AND WATCHMAKER ON THE DERBY

SINCE THE BEYER SPEED FIGURES are such an important piece of the puzzle for predicting the contenders for the Kentucky Oaks and Derby, it seemed logical to get an expert perspective from Andrew Beyer himself, who provided the following answers to questions regarding his speed figures and their importance in analyzing horse racing's most challenging 3-year-old contests. *Daily Racing Form* national handicapper Mike Watchmaker, who spends a great deal of time studying various handicapping patterns of big-race-day events, also provided his input on the topic.

1. How important are the Beyer Speed Figures in determining the winners of the Oaks and the Derby? Are there any distinct Beyer patterns that you've noticed over the years that the bettor should be aware of when evaluating the speed figures of these developing 3-year-olds?

Andrew Beyer: *A horse's raw ability has become more important than the extent of his preparation, and speed figures have become the key factor in handicapping the Derby. Since 1990, the mean winning Beyer*

Speed Figure for the Derby has been 108. In eight of the last 11 years, the winner had earned a figure of 108 or higher before the first Saturday in May. Handicappers don't need to be this stringent in deciding who is a legitimate contender, but it is a reasonable rule of thumb to eliminate any horse who hasn't run at least a 102 before the Derby. (In recent years, only Giacomo in 2005 and Sea Hero in 1993 have failed to meet this guideline.)

Mike Watchmaker: Regarding Beyer Speed Figures in the Derby, or the Oaks, for that matter, it is important to remember that you are dealing with young 3-year-olds who can improve significantly practically overnight, improvement that can be reflected in the figures they earn. These young 3-year-olds for the most part haven't yet established a ceiling to their abilities. Another thing to remember is to not split hairs and take the Beyers too literally. To say that a colt who earned a 107 last time out has to beat one who earned a 105 last time out is a mistake, because it is important to consider the context in which those Beyers were earned. (Perfect trip? Against a track bias?) That goes for every race, not just the Derby. One thing I like to do with Beyers in not just the Derby or Oaks, but any race, is to use them to eliminate horses who are just simply too slow to win. This is a perfectly valid handicapping approach, as sometimes you can throw out a huge chunk of the field.

2. Besides evaluating a horse's speed figures, are there any other handicapping tools that you can share with the public that constitute a winning Derby profile? As bettors, should we be looking at the number of prep races, stakes wins, or success at nine furlongs in determining whether a specific 3-year-old is likely to get the distance?

Andrew Beyer: Over the years, trainers' methods of preparing horses for the Kentucky Derby have changed dramatically. And the process of handicapping the Derby has changed, too.

I used to believe that the nature of a horse's overall preparation was more important than his speed figures. It was essential for a colt to have extensive experience to be fit for the Derby. He should have had a solid 2-year-old campaign and three or four prep races as a 3-year-old. Lightly raced horses and late bloomers rarely succeeded.

As Thoroughbreds have become less durable, trainers now like to bring horses into stakes races "fresh." Colts now come into the Derby *with light campaigns that would have been unimaginable in the past. It used to be a rule that a horse needed a prep race within four weeks of the Derby—and then Barbaro won after a five-week layoff in 2006. Only one of the old handicapping guidelines has held up. A horse must have raced as a 2-year-old in order to be a viable contender. (Without a foundation of 2-year-old experience, no horse has won the Derby since 1882.) But most of the old rules governing the necessary pre-Derby preparation are now irrelevant.*

Mike Watchmaker: *We've seen in the last two years with Barbaro and Street Sense a huge alteration of the old "Derby Rules," some of which mandated recent activity within four weeks, or at least three prep races at 3. While it looks like these rules no longer apply, it is important to remember that they generally resulted in a fit horse with a solid foundation. I'm not sure fitness and seasoning will ever fall by the wayside, especially in as demanding a race as the Derby. But it may take on new and different forms.*

3. What would be your best advice to the handicapper looking to make a betting assault on Oaks and Derby Day? Are there many amateur-bettor pitfalls to avoid?

Andrew Beyer: *Often the betting public gets so caught up in pre-Derby hype that it overlooks the horse who has earned the best Beyer Speed Figure in his most recent start. In run-of-the-mill races, such horses are almost always heavily bet. But in 2002, War Emblem came into the Derby after running a figure of 112 in his prior start and won, paying $43. In 1999 Charismatic was one of two entrants who had a last-race figure of 108; he won and paid $64.60. In 1992, Lil E. Tee had the co-best last-race figure and paid $35.60. The results suggest that it might pay for handicappers to eschew subtleties when analyzing the Derby and look for the fastest horse.*

Mike Watchmaker: *The best advice I can offer is to be patient. Be very, very patient. While I firmly believe sometimes one's biggest scores come in races they might not have originally been crazy about, there is so much time between races on these days that it is often easy to become financially involved in a race that you really shouldn't have been involved in at all.*

WHAT IS A BEYER PAR?

A BEYER PAR is the average winning Beyer Speed Figure for a particular class level. In the case of the Kentucky Derby, we can take a look at the past Beyer numbers earned by previous Derby winners and get an idea of the average number, or par, that is usually required to win the race. We can then study the past performances for the current year's Derby contenders and determine which of the entrants have already achieved the Derby par—or better yet, which ones might be improving enough to run a number that can win.

Daily Racing Form started printing Beyer Speed Figures in 1992, which allows us a clean and adequate 16-year sample to evaluate the winning numbers. Below are the last 16 Derby winners, culminating with Street Sense in 2007, and their respective Beyer Speed Figures.

Derby Winner	Year	Beyer Speed Figure
Street Sense	(2007)	110
Barbaro	(2006)	111
Giacomo	(2005)	100
Smarty Jones	(2004)	107
Funny Cide	(2003)	109
War Emblem	(2002)	114
Monarchos	(2001)	116
Fusaichi Pegasus	(2000)	108
Charismatic	(1999)	108
Real Quiet	(1998)	107
Silver Charm	(1997)	115
Grindstone	(1996)	112
Thunder Gulch	(1995)	108
Go For Gin	(1994)	112
Sea Hero	(1993)	105
Lil E. Tee	(1992)	107

Average Winning Derby Beyer: **109**

Now that we have established that the Beyer par for what it takes to win the Kentucky Derby is 109, we may be able to uncover some hidden clues or patterns for potential winners—or, at the very least, solid contenders—based on the numbers they've run prior to the big race. Let's look at the last three Beyer Speed Figures of each of the last 16 Derby winners and see if there are patterns we can expose and use to our advantage when wagering. Which horses had already earned the 109 winning Derby par even before the race?

*Each Beyer Speed Figure that reached or exceeded 100 is indicated in bold.

		Prior to Derby	Two Back	Three Back
Street Sense	(2007)	93	**102**	**108**
Barbaro	(2006)	**103**	95	97
Giacomo	(2005)	95	93	98
Smarty Jones	(2004)	**109**	**112**	95
Funny Cide	(2003)	**110**	99	87
War Emblem	(2002)	**112**	98	85
Monarchos	(2001)	**103**	**105**	**103**
Fusaichi Pegasus	(2000)	**111**	**106**	**103**
Charismatic	(1999)	**108**	94	95
Real Quiet	(1998)	**107**	**108**	59
Silver Charm	(1997)	**110**	**102**	**110**
Grindstone	(1996)	**100**	**102**	92

		Prior to Derby	Two Back	Three Back
Thunder Gulch	(1995)	**101**	**101**	**105**
Go For Gin	(1994)	**107**	**104**	98
Sea Hero	(1993)	91	91	66
Lil E. Tee	(1992)	**107**	95	**106**

Another point to consider is that out of the 16 Kentucky Derby winners listed above, 87 percent had reached or exceeded a Beyer Speed Figure of 100 in one of their three starts preceding the Derby. Why is this significant? As the chart below indicates, there have only been two Derby winners in the last 16 years—Giacomo in 2005 and Sea Hero in 1993—who had not cracked 100 before the big race itself. (Sea Hero ran his career top of 99, shown below, as a 2-year-old in the Champagne Stakes, not in one of his Derby preps.) This is crucial handicapping data to keep in mind when look-ing at the past performances for your next Kentucky Derby.

HIGHEST WINNING PRE-DERBY BEYER SPEED FIGURE		
Street Sense	(2007)	108
Barbaro	(2006)	103
Giacomo	(2005)	98
Smarty Jones	(2004)	112
Funny Cide	(2003)	110
War Emblem	(2002)	112
Monarchos	(2001)	105
Fusaichi Pegasus	(2000)	111
Charismatic	(1999)	108
Real Quiet	(1998)	108
Silver Charm	(1997)	110
Grindstone	(1996)	102
Thunder Gulch	(1995)	105
Go For Gin	(1994)	107
Sea Hero	(1993)	99
Lil E. Tee	(1992)	107
Average Pre-Derby Beyer		**106.9**

As noted earlier, however, there's usually more to successful hand-icapping than just betting the horse with the highest Beyer Speed Figure. That holds especially true when handicapping the Kentucky Derby, a race with a wide variety of unknowns and variables to take into account. Out of the last 16 runnings, only five have been won by the horse with the highest or co-highest Beyer: Street Sense (108) in 2007; War Emblem (112) in 2002; Fusaichi Pegasus (111) in 2000; Charismatic (108) in 1999; and Lil E. Tee (107) in 1992.

If it's not just a matter of betting the horse with the biggest num-ber, where do you turn? One of the things that makes handicap-ping the Derby so challenging—and potentially so rewarding—is trying to determine which horses are improving. That improvement can be sudden, as Mike Watchmaker noted earlier, but it can also be gradual. While some young 3-year-olds might take a giant leap forward from one race to the next, it is quite common for others to show a steady, step-by-step increase in their Beyer Speed Figures. This particular Beyer pattern has produced several Derby winners. Although the sequence isn't always perfect, the following nine horses provide a solid example of how projecting Beyer improvement in still-developing 3-year-olds can be profitable.

	Derby Beyer	Prior to Derby	Two Back	Three Back
Barbaro	**111**	103	95	97
Giacomo	**100**	95	93	98
Funny Cide	**109**	110	99	87
War Emblem	**114**	112	98	85
Silver Charm	**115**	110	102	110
Grindstone	**112**	100	102	92
Thunder Gulch	**108**	101	101	105
Go For Gin	**112**	107	104	98
Sea Hero	**105**	91	91	66

3

CHURCHILL DOWNS POST POSITIONS AND TRACK BIAS: MYTHS VS. REALITY

*T*HE DRAW FOR post positions, a random procedure that takes place after entries for a race are submitted, can often turn a potential winner into a dead loser, and vice versa. The simplest kind of track bias to understand is the post-position bias, in which certain posts become advantageous at certain distances.

Track biases exist at many tracks, favoring inside or outside post positions. Post-position biases are also referred to as track profiles, which is a convenient way to differentiate a permanent post-position profile from temporary pace and lane biases. Post-position biases, if they exist, usually are due to starting-gate placement and occasionally are a result of changing weather conditions associated with temperature and moisture. In most scenarios, races that start too close to a turn favor inside posts. Conversely, outside posts are disadvantageous in races that start too close to a turn. But post-position biases can also be caused by other factors. For example, a track that has a deeper or looser cushion near the rail could be biased, since horses that have drawn the inside post positions will have a more difficult time breaking sharply.

The most advantageous bias for handicappers is the severe positive speed bias inside, or on the rail. The positive inside-speed bias propels any horse with a trace of speed to the front, and often sustains him to the wire unchallenged. A classic example of an incredible inside-speed bias on the main dirt track occurred during the 2006 running of the Breeders' Cup at Churchill Downs. Four of the five Cup races on the dirt that day were won by the horse breaking from post 1, including longshots Street Sense ($32.40) in the Juvenile, Thor's Echo ($33.20) in the Sprint, and Round Pond ($29.80) in the Distaff. This was not an illusion or coincidence, and paid great dividends for those who caught on early in the afternoon and were sharp enough to adjust their selections.

The opposite bias, a severe negative-inside-speed bias, hinders horses exiting the rail post. Outside biases, positive or negative, can be equally as severe as inside biases, and can impact several post positions. Sometimes horses in the far-outside posts might have an atypical advantage; it all depends on a variety of factors. Sound confusing?

Although track biases occur with regularity, they are often misunderstood by casual fans and even by some seasoned racegoers. It is quite common for fans to learn of track biases and then go overboard in trying to identify them and use them in their handicapping.

Post-position studies published by *Daily Racing Form* and in track programs can alert handicappers to the inside-outside biases currently operating at their home tracks, and it pays to keep abreast of any unusual trends. Severe biases can represent outstanding sources of financial gain, whether during the course of a day, a weekend, a week, a few weeks, or, if you're very lucky, occasionally as much as a month. It pays to scrutinize biases closely enough to detect when a predominant pattern may be settling in.

The same can be said of analyzing past Derby post positions and how they have fared. Early speed is usually preferable for both inside and outside posts because without it, horses on the outside can lose ground and the ones on the inside can get trapped in traffic. As a general rule, though, the closer to the rail a horse starts, the better his chances of success, and in a bulky field, the two outside posts can be a real disadvantage. An inside post makes it easier for a horse to get good early position. The logic seems simple enough. Or is it?

A horse's running style and the post position are directly related. In longer, two-turn races such as the Kentucky Derby, it might seem that inside posts would almost always be preferred, but history has proven time and time again that that is not always the case. The 1986 Kentucky Derby winner, Ferdinand, and the 1963 victor, Chateaugay, both started from post 1, and they remain the only two colts to win from the inside slot in the last 45 years.

How do we know if a track has a post-position bias, specifically Churchill Downs on Kentucky Derby Day? Are most casual handicapping theorists correct in thinking that outside post positions place horses at a disadvantage? Does this apparent disadvantage more correctly result from how far a horse is from the rail when he gets to the turn? What is the disadvantage of racing wide on a turn? Can this disadvantage be predicted by pace and running style and then quantified in Beyer Speed Figures? And, how can knowledge of this disadvantage be turned into a betting advantage?

Below is a post-position study of the last 38 runnings of the Kentucky Derby, starting with the 1970 winner, Dust Commander. Here is the rundown indicating total wins by post position.

Wins by Post Position	
Distance: 1¼ miles, main track	
Post 1:	1
Post 2:	4
Post 3:	4
Post 4:	1
Post 5:	4
Post 6:	1
Post 7:	2
Post 8:	3
Post 9:	1
Post 10:	7
Post 11:	1
Post 12:	1
Post 13:	1
Post 14:	0
Post 15:	3
Post 16:	3
Post 17:	0
Post 18:	1
Post 19:	0

(continued)

Wins by Post Position Distance: 1 1/4 miles, main track	
Post 20:	0
Post 21:	0
Post 22:	0
Post 23:	0

If you were to follow this post-position table, hoping to gain insight into which Derby slots produce the most winners, you'd be heading in the wrong handicapping direction. What's wrong with this table, or, more correctly, what was wrong with the way this information was accumulated?

You've probably observed that the number of wins tended to decline as we progressed to the far-outside post positions. Does that mean there is a bias in favor of the inside posts and against the outside posts at Churchill Downs? We don't know for sure, and having just this retrievable data on hand is not sufficient and reliable.

Here's one reason we cannot make any conclusions based on the information in the above table. It is very possible that the number of wins declined because there were *fewer overall starters in the outermost post positions*. Therefore, the far-outside posts could not have been expected to produce as many winners. We have identified the first error in the construction of the above table: *The data fails to take into account the number of starters from each post position*. Another thing to keep in mind is that it is possible that a track could have a post-position bias in effect for races at one distance and not at another distance.

For several years, the consensus among so-called handicapping experts as well as the general public was that outside post positions were taboo, and there was some data to support this theory. Horses breaking from the auxiliary gate (post 15 and higher) are a combined 7 for 133 in the history of the race, but five of those wins have occurred within the last 12 years. The rigid belief that "the outside post is not the best place to be" started to crack with the 1995 running of the Derby, when Thunder Gulch scored from post 16 and paid $51.

EIGHTH RACE 1¼ MILES. (1.59²) KENTUCKY DERBY Grade I. Purse $500,000

Churchill

MAY 6, 1995

Value of Race: $957,400 Winner $707,400; second $145,000; third $70,000; fourth $35,000. Mutuel Pool $12,851,173.00 Exacta Pool $5,476,539.00 Trifecta Pool $3,921,394.00

Last Raced	Horse	M/Eqt.	A.	Wt	PP	¼	½	¾	1	Str	Fin	Jockey	Odds $1
15Apr95 7Kee⁴	Thunder Gulch	b	3	126	16	6¹½	5½	4ʰᵈ	2ʰᵈ	1²	12¼	Stevens G L	24.50
15Apr95 7Kee³	Tejano Run	L	3	126	14	12½	12½	11½	8½	31½	2ʰᵈ	Bailey J D	8.60
8Apr95 5SA⁴	Timber Country		3	126	15	14¹½	13ʰᵈ	10ʰᵈ	10ʰᵈ	6ʰᵈ	3¾	Day P	x- 3.40
8Apr95 5SA³	Jumron-GB	L	3	126	10	8½	9¹½	9¹½	4½	5½	4ʰᵈ	Almeida G F	5.60
23Apr95 11Hia²	Mecke	L b	3	126	18	17½	16¹	1⁹	14²	7¹	5½	Davis R G	11.60
20Apr95 8NEW³	Eltish		3	126	7	10½	10½	13½	9ʰᵈ	9¹½	6³	Delahoussaye E	10.90
15Apr95 9Aqu⁸	Knockadoon		3	126	2	1⁹	1⁹	18ʰᵈ	13½	11½	7ⁿᵏ	McCarron C J	11.60
8Apr95 5SA²	Afternoon Deelites		3	126	12	7½	8½	6½	5¹½	10ʰᵈ	8ⁿᵏ	Desormeaux K J	8.70
19Apr95 NEW³	Citadeed	L	3	126	19	3½	4¹	3¹	6½	8½	9¾	Maple E	11.60
8Apr95 5SA⁶	In Character-GB	L	3	126	9	16½	15¹	15ʰᵈ	12ʰᵈ	13²	10½	Antley C W	11.60
15Apr95 7Kee²	Suave Prospect	L	3	126	6	9½	11²	12ʰᵈ	7½	12¹½	11½	Krone J A	13.10
15Apr95 9Aqu¹	Talkin Man		3	126	11	4¹½	3ʰᵈ	5¹	3¹½	2ʰᵈ	12½	Smith M E	4.00
22Apr95 9OP¹	Dazzling Falls	L b	3	126	1	13ʰᵈ	14¹	17½	18⁴	16²	13ⁿᵏ	Gomez G K	27.60
5Feb95 11Kyo¹	Ski Captain		3	126	17	18½	17½	16ʰᵈ	15½	14¹½	14¹½	Take Y	11.60
15Apr95 7Kee⁵	Jambalaya Jazz	L	3	126	5	15½	18¹½	14¹	17¹½	15ʰᵈ	15ⁿᵏ	Perret C	x- 18.00
1Apr95 11TP¹	Serena's Song		3	121	13	1½	1¹	1¹	1¹	4ʰᵈ	16¹½	Nakatani C S	x- 3.40
1Apr95 10Hia¹	Pyramid Peak		3	126	3	5ʰᵈ	6ʰᵈ	8ʰᵈ	11ʰᵈ	17⁵	17⁶	McCauley W H	x- 18.00
8Apr95 5SA⁵	Lake George	L	3	126	8	11¹½	7½	7½	16²	18¹²	18²¹	Sellers S J	11.60
15Apr95 7Kee¹	Wild Syn	L	3	126	4	2½	2¹½	2ʰᵈ	1⁹	1⁹	1⁹	Romero R P	18.80

x–Coupled: Timber Country and Jambalaya Jazz and Serena's Song and Pyramid Peak.

OFF AT 5:33 Start Good For All But . Won . Track fast.

TIME :22², :45⁴, 1:10¹, 1:35³, 2:01¹ (:22.57, :45.89, 1:10.33, 1:35.72, 2:01.27)

$2 Mutuel Prices:	11 – THUNDER GULCH....................	51.00	24.20	12.20
	10 – TEJANO RUN.......................		10.20	6.80
	2B– TIMBER COUNTRY(x–entry)..........			3.80

$2 EXACTA 11–10 PAID $480.00 $1 TRIFECTA 11–10–2 PAID $2,099.20

Ch. c, (May), by Gulch – Line of Thunder , by Storm Bird . Trainer Lukas D Wayne. Bred by Peter M Brant (Ky).

The outside-post-position parade continued in 1996 with Grindstone (post 15; $13.80), followed by 1999 winner Charismatic (post 16; $64.60), 2000 winner Fusaichi Pegasus (post 15; $6.60), 2001 victor Monarchos (post 16; $23), and most recently 2004 winner Smarty Jones (post 13; $10.20). It had become apparent that an outside post, in the absence of any other considerations, was less of a factor, and a specific entrant's running style was much more important. It's safe to say, that horses with natural speed and other need-the-lead types and stalkers (horses that like to run a few lengths off the front-runners) are the ones who are compromised the most by an outside draw. Closers (horses that need to be off the pace) must avoid being caught wide on the first turn, and their jockeys should find a comfortable spot as close to the rail as possible in order to save ground.

A more reliable and useful Kentucky Derby post-position analysis involves not only tracking the winner, but also looking at the other horses that filled out the exacta, trifecta, and superfecta. Let's examine the post-position results for the same 38 runnings of the Kentucky Derby since 1970, using a more comprehensive analysis.

*Average starters: 16.57
*Largest field: 23 (1974, Cannonade)
*Smallest Field: 9 (1976, Bold Forbes)

Post	Starts	Win	Place	Show	4th	Win %	ITM %	Super ITM %
1	38	1	0	4	4	2%	13%	24%
2	38	4	1	4	0	10%	24%	24%
3	38	4	2	4	2	10%	26%	32%
4	38	1	5	1	4	2%	18%	29%
5	38	4	3	0	4	10%	18%	29%
6	38	1	2	0	1	2%	8%	11%
7	38	2	1	1	6	5%	11%	26%
8	38	3	3	3	4	8%	24%	34%
9	38	1	1	3	3	2%	13%	21%
10	**37**	**7**	**3**	**4**	**2**	**19%**	**38%**	**43%**
11	36	1	2	1	0	3%	11%	11%
12	35	1	2	2	1	3%	14%	17%
13	35	1	4	4	4	3%	25%	37%
14	31	0	2	3	1	0%	16%	19%
15	30	3	1	1	0	10%	16%	16%
16	25	3	1	2	0	12%	24%	24%
17	20	0	1	0	1	0%	5%	10%
18	17	1	3	0	0	6%	24%	24%
19	14	0	1	0	0	0%	7%	7%
20	8	0	0	1	1	0%	13%	25%
21	2	0	0	0	0	0%	0%	0%
22	1	0	0	0	0	0%	0%	0%
23	1	0	0	0	0	0%	0%	0%

A quick analysis uncovers that post 10 has been the liveliest with nearly 20 percent winners, 38 percent in-the-money finishes, and horses filling out the last superfecta slot at 43 percent. It's also interesting that post 1 has resulted in only one win-and-place finish in more than three decades of racing.

What does this all mean, and how does it factor into wagering on the Kentucky Derby? If you have a Derby selection that has drawn one of the unfavorable post-position slots, don't dismiss his chances solely because of the unflattering draw. There are many other important handicapping factors that are just as significant, and it's more beneficial to attempt to determine what type of trip your selection may have, based on his past running style and where he's breaking from this afternoon.

4

TOMLINSON RATINGS AND PEDIGREE HANDICAPPING

PEDIGREE BECOMES AN important factor when handicapping the Kentucky Derby or on any other racing day when attempting to determine how a specific horse will perform while trying something for the first time. A horse's success can have a lot to do with how his sire and dam handled the same circumstances, because they pass on certain characteristics to their offspring.

Pedigree handicapping provides a clue to a horse's potential to handle an unfamiliar surface or distance and determines what type of running style he or she is likely to possess. This is a major consideration when a horse attempts something for either the first or second time in his career. For example, how will a horse perform on a muddy or sloppy surface, or how will he handle the turf course? Is he best suited to a sprint, a middle-distance event, or a marathon? As a handicapper you hope to gain some insight based on bloodlines.

Invariably, pedigree analysis becomes one of the hottest topics of conversation in the days and weeks leading up to the Derby, when horseplayers are attempting to determine how a large group of lightly raced 3-year-olds might adjust and perform when confronted with the grueling 1¹/4-mile distance for the first time, and how they might react if the track comes up sloppy on the first Saturday in May.

TOMLINSON RATINGS

LEE TOMLINSON is the founder and creator of Tomlinson Ratings. He began his rating and pedigree study over 20 years ago after suffering through one too many losing days at the track when inclement weather turned the surface to slop. Tomlinson began the scholarly task of poring over several thousand copies of old *Daily Racing Forms* and result charts, hoping to uncover some pedigree data that could be directly linked to a horse's performance on wet tracks. He came up with a list of sires whose offspring were more likely to handle off tracks, and eventually did the same for turf and distance sires.

Through Tomlinson's extensive research, it soon became clear that pedigree was indeed relevant in determining how a specific horse might perform on a wet track, the turf, or over a specific distance of ground. The Tomlinson Ratings were born in two original retail products known and sold as "Mudders & Turfers" and "Sprinters & Stayers." The original numbers began to take form using the antiquated pen-and-pencil method, but were later modernized when a huge computerized database was created. A few years later, the wet-track ratings were adopted into the lifetime-record segment of *Daily Racing Form* past performances, followed by the turf and distance ratings.

In addition to the Tomlinson Ratings, which project how a horse might perform on a certain surface, *Daily Racing Form* also shows a horse's record on off tracks in his career box in the PPs. Years ago, before these innovations, the *Racing Form* did not show the wet-track record for each runner; instead, a symbol, or "mud mark," was placed just under the horse's name to indicate whether that runner was "fair," "good," or "superior" on off tracks. This revealed whether the horse had already shown the ability to handle a muddy or sloppy surface, but there was no information at all for those horses who had never run on an off track. And this is where the value lies in Tomlinson's pedigree-driven numerical creation.

Today, Tomlinson Ratings are carried exclusively in *Daily Racing*

Form past performances, and they offer a measure of potential in two other areas besides how a horse might run on a wet track: turf and distance of ground. The Tomlinson distance rating frequently provides a clue as to which runners have the staying power to excel at the longer classic distances.

reet Sense
: Jim Tafel LLC

Dk. b or b. c. 3 (Feb)
Sire: Street Cry*Ire (Machiavellian) $30,000
Dam: Bedazzle (Dixieland Band)
Br: James Tafel (Ky)
Tr: Nafzger Carl A(0 0 0 0 .00) 2007:(77 18 .23)

Life	13	6	4	2	$4,383,200	111	D.Fst	8	6	2	0	$3,836,200	111
2007	8	4	3	0	$3,205,000	111	Wet(378)	2	0	0	1	$277,000	104
							Synth	3	0	2	1	$270,000	107
2006	5	2	1	2	$1,178,200	108	Turf(309)	0	0	0	0	$0	-
	0	0	0	0	$0	-	Dst(297*)	0	0	0	0	$0	-

ct07-11Mth	slyS	1¼		:454	1:103	1:354	2:002	3↑BCClasic-G1	104	2	711	67½	34	33½	410¼	Borel C H	L121 f	*2.50	106- 07 Curlin1214½ Hard Spun1214¾ Awesome Gem1261	Inside, no winning bid	9
ep07-10TP	fst	1⅛	◈	:48	1:112	1:353	1:482	3↑KyCpCls-G2	107	3	21	21	21	2½	21¼	Borel C H	L120 f	*.80	98- 08 HardSpun1181¼ StreetSense1203¼ StreamCat11811¼	Bid, gamely, 2nd best	4
g07- 9Sar	fst	1¼		:48	1:122	1:364	2:023	Travers-G1	108	4	31½	31	2hd	1hd	1½	Borel C H	L126 f	*.35	91- 09 Street Sense126½ Grasshopper12610¼ Helsinki126nk	Determined outside	7
y07- 9Sar	fst	1⅛		:47	1:113	1:361	1:484	JimDandy-G2	105	3	53½	53	41	2hd	11½	Borel C H	L123 f	*.35	93- 07 *Street Sense*1231½ C P West115¾ Sightseeing1211½	When roused, clear	6
ay07-12Pim	fst	1 3/16		:453	1:094	1:343	1:532	Preaknes-G1	111	8	89½	815	79½	11½	2hd	Borel C H	L126 f	*1.30	105- 05 Curlin126hd *Street Sense*1264 Hard Spun1261½	Swung 4wide, yielded	9
ay07-10CD	fst	1¼		:461	1:11	1:37	2:02	KyDerby-G1	110	7	1919	1712	33½	11	12¼	Borel C H	L126 f	*4.90	96- 09 Street Sense1262¼ Hard Spun1265¾ *Curlin*126½	Rail to lane,split,drv	20
pr07- 9Kee	fst	1⅛	◈	:512	1:163	1:394	1:511	BlueGras-G1	93	4	42½	42½	42	4¾	2no	Borel C H	L123 f	*1.10	88- 15 Dominican123no *Street Sense*123hd Zanjero123hd	Floated out 3/16s	7
ar07-12Tam	fst	1 1/16		:232	:472	1:12	1:43	TampaDby-G3	102	2	46½	47	44½	1½	1no	Borel C H	L122 f	1.20	100- 10 StrtSns122no AnyGivnSturdy1206¼ DlghtfulKss1162	Dueled,brushd,all out	7

Every horse whose sire and maternal grandsire (damsire) have had a meaningful sample of offspring is assigned two Tomlinson Ratings—one that assesses his likely aptitude for grass and one that does the same thing for muddy or sloppy tracks. These ratings, which are updated quarterly, are derived from an analysis of tens of thousands of race results on turf courses or wet tracks. The ratings, which appear next to the "Turf" and "Wet" headings in each horse's career box, can range from 0 (totally unsuccessful) to 480 (spectacularly successful.) A dash (-) means that the horse's sire has not had a sufficient number of runners to create a rating.

Runners whose sire and/or damsire have relatively small samples (fewer than 80 runners) are listed with an asterisk (*) following the rating. As with all statistical studies, small samples must be regarded with caution. In fact, I would be inclined to favor a solid rating of, let's say, 380, over a rating of 400 that has an asterisk attached.

The following are some general rating guidelines presented by *Daily Racing Form* with the help of Lee Tomlinson himself.

MUDDERS & TURFERS RATINGS

Mud Rating of 320+ Merits further consideration as a horse that could run particularly well over a wet track.

Turf Rating of 280+ Merits further consideration as a horse that could run particularly well over the grass.

If properly utilized and combined with other modern handicapping methods, these ratings can be extremely useful, especially in the following race-day circumstances:

1. In most 2-year-old maiden races where horses have limited starts and are more likely to be trying an off track, the grass, or a distance of ground for the first or second time.
2. Any race that was switched from an originally scheduled turf event to a main track listed as "sloppy" or "muddy."
3. Any other race where a horse might be trying the mud, slop, turf, or a distance of ground for the first or second time.

Once a runner has raced more than three times on the same surface he faces today, he has most likely given an indication as to whether he likes or dislikes it. The key in any given race is not so much what horse has the highest rating overall, but rather the difference, or margin, that separates the contenders, providing that the runner with the highest rating "merits further consideration." When the margin in question is 40 points or more on mud/slop, and 30 points or more on turf, it pays to take extra notice of this particular runner.

TOMLINSON DISTANCE RATINGS

DAILY RACING FORM has also added the Tomlinson Distance Ratings to the career box above each horse's past performances. These are based on a statistical analysis of the performance of other Thoroughbreds with the same pedigree influences, and may prove helpful in predicting a horse's ability to handle the distance of today's race.

These ratings, which appear in parentheses after the abbreviation "Dst" in the career box, are similar to the Tomlinson Wet-Track and Turf Ratings, which already appear in the box. Ratings range from 0 to 480, with a rating of around 320 considered average. A rating followed by an asterisk means the number is based on a small data sample, usually because a sire or damsire has had a limited number of runners.

Unlike the other Tomlinson Ratings, the Distance Ratings are keyed to the distance of the race in which the horse is entered today. Races fall into one of four categories: six furlongs or shorter; more than six furlongs but less than a mile; a mile or more but less than a mile and a quarter; and a mile and a quarter and longer. Each horse has a rating, revised quarterly, in each of the four distance categories, and the one that appears today is determined by the distance of today's race.

These ratings might prove especially useful when handicapping younger horses with a limited number of starts at the distance in question. What race fits that description like a glove? You guessed it—the Kentucky Derby.

Here are two examples of "question mark" situations where the ratings should provide considerable help. In the Kentucky Derby you're looking at a field of 3-year-olds scheduled to go $1^1/4$ miles. Although several entrants have gone $1^1/8$ miles, none has ever been that extra furlong. A look at the ratings might give you a clue as to which of today's contestants has the pedigree to get the distance.

WINNING DERBY SIRES

THE WINNER OF the Kentucky Derby usually has a combination of natural ability and the bloodlines to be effective at $1^1/4$ miles. In recent decades, however, many North American Thoroughbred farms have begun to breed for speed rather than stamina, catering to the economics of the game and the win-early attitude of many owners. The end result has been a turning of the tide where precocious pedigrees have begun to sneak into some of the most recent Derby winners' profiles.

A stamina-oriented pedigree used to be very important in the Derby. If a horse had the bloodlines of a sprinter, you could eliminate him even if his form looked favorable. But now there are very few true $1^1/4$-mile horses bred in this country, and runners with sprint-oriented pedigrees can win America's greatest race. Some recent winners with more of a sprinter/miler pedigree that come to mind include: Giacomo (2005), Smarty Jones (2004), Funny Cide (2003), and War Emblem (2002). Recent winners Street Sense (2007) and Barbaro (2006) were more representative of the traditional stamina-driven dirt influences in a Derby winner's pedigree.

American dirt racing has seen fewer and fewer long-distance events on the main track, and this could be contributing to the decline of marathon pedigrees and runners as well. Compounding the problem is the fact that many of the best stallion and broodmare prospects of the last few decades have been purchased by European, Middle Eastern, and Japanese interests and taken out of the country. Despite a changing of the guard that has seen more sprinter/miler pedigrees showing up among the winners of American classic races, the value of recognizing stallions that have proven progeny at marathon dirt distances should not be overlooked or undervalued.

Following is a list of sires who succeeded at classic distances and/or in the Kentucky Derby itself. Their offspring should be given extra consideration if they happen to turn up in upcoming Derby past performances. Those highlighted in bold won the Kentucky Derby.

Affirmed
Alleged
Alphabet Soup
A.P. Indy
Arch
Baldski
Barathea (Ire)
Bluebird
Boundary
Broad Brush
Candy Stripes
Capote
Conquistador Cielo
Cozzene
Danehill
Danzig
Deputy Commander
Deputy Minister
Distorted Humor
Dixieland Band
El Prado
Empire Maker
Giant's Causeway
Gold Fever

Gone West
Kingmambo
Kris S.
Langfuhr
Lemon Drop Kid
Maria's Mon
Milwaukee Brew
Monarchos
Mutakddim
Nijinsky II
Not for Love
Pine Bluff
Pleasant Colony
Rahy
Runaway Groom
Sadler's Wells
Sea Hero
Seattle Slew
Seeking the Gold
Smarty Jones
Silver Charm
Sky Classic
Smart Strike
Spend a Buck
Storm Cat
Street Cry
Strike the Gold
Thunder Gulch
Unbridled
Unbridled's Song

5

THE RELIABILITY OF
PRE-DERBY WORKOUTS

HORSES WORK OUT in the morning to prepare for upcoming races. The most recent workouts are found under each horse's past performances. Take a look at the past performances for the 6-year-old turf gelding Toasted on the next page and see if you can follow along with his last work tab, which culminated with a move on November 12 at Hollywood Park.

Workouts list the date (Nov12), the track or training facility (in this case "Hol," which is Hollywood Park), the distance in furlongs (4f), track condition (fst means fast), time (:49³), and the clocker's comment ("H" means handily, indicating the horse was under urging from his rider during the workout, whereas a "B" would mean breezing, indicating the horse wasn't under strong urging). The numbers that follow the H (41/48) show where that morning drill ranked in relation to the other horses who worked the same distance at that track on that day. There are up to six workouts listed for horses that have previously raced and up to 12 for first-time starters. A bullet (•) indicates the fastest workout of the day at the track and distance. Toasted shows a bullet workout on September 29. Note: Other abbreviations include "g," which indicates the horse worked

5 Toasted
Own: Robert D. Bone
8–5 Black, gold crown emblem on back, gold
Gomez G K (62 14 17 5 .22) 2007:(1150 238 .21)

Dk. b or br g. 6 (Apr)
Sire: Hennessy (Storm Cat) $60,000
Dam: Burrows (Seattle Song)
Br: James D. Haley(Ky)
Tr: Mitchell Mike (19 5 7 2 .26) 2007:(294 66 .22)

L 120

Life	25	5	5	6	$516,812	105	D.Fst	1	0	0	0		
2007	9	0	3	1	$79,547	99	Wet (329)	0	0	0	0		
2006	5	1	0	2	$74,094	105	Turf (319)	24	5	5	6	$516	
Hol Ⓣ	3	0	1	1	$33,160	93	Dist (365)	2	1	1	0	$139	

17Nov07-8Hol fm 1⅛Ⓣ:50 1:134 1:363 1:481 + 3↑OC 150k/N$MY 93 7 63½ 63½ 75 64¾ 32¾ Nakatani C S LB124b 4.30 77-16 StormMltry1202 Obrgdo124¾ Tostd1241¼ 3wd into str,miss
13Oct07-7OSAfm 1 Ⓣ:234 :474 1:112 1:351 3↑[R]WarChant67k 92 4 65½ 76 65½ 64¼ 72½ Nakatani C S LB119 2.60 85-09 StrmnAy124¾ *StrmMltr* 118nk *LngFld* 118hd acked room 1/8 &
6Oct07-9OSAfm 1¼Ⓣ:4811:121 1:36 1:594 3↑CLHirsch-G1 99 4 42½ 42 31½ 43 53 Baze M C LB124 6.20 89-12 ArtistRoyl1241 ThTinMn124nk Ispngo1241 3wd into str,wk
26Aug07-7Dmrfm 1⅜Ⓣ:4811:123 1:362 2:13 3↑DelMarH-G2 97 6 23½ 23 43 43 4¾ Baze M C LB115b 9.20 94-08 AftrMrkt124¾ RnwyDncr118no *SprngHs* 115no 3wd into str,w
1Aug07-2Dmrfm 1⅜Ⓣ:4921:141 1:371 2:13 3↑[R]CougarIIH88k 94 2 53½ 65¾ 67¾ 41¾ 21½ Baze M C LB117b 2.80 93-08 AtIndo1181½ Tosted1171 BrvoMestro1153½ 4wd into lane,r
Previously trained by Ford Jeff 2007(as of 5/5):(3 1 1 0 0.33)
5May07-6AP gd 1$\frac{1}{16}$Ⓣ:242 :491 1:132 1:44 3↑[R]IlOwners100k 96 1 53 63½ 62¾ 3½ 2½ Douglas R R L116 2.50 87-14 FortPrdo118½ Tosted1164½ LordCrmen118no Late rally, m
Previously trained by De Seroux Laura 2006:(74 3 8 15 0.04)
3Mar07 11SA fm 1⅛Ⓣ:50 1:141 1:373 1:483 4↑Alw 84600N$MY 83 3 63½ 75½ 84¼ 86¼ 87½ Valdivia J Jr LB118 9.90 77-10 *IcyAtlantic* 1182 Rilrod123nk Crested1181½ Chased btwn,no
3Feb07-8SA fm 1 Ⓣ:241 :49 1:12 1:352 4↑ThunderRdH80k 97 8 45 65¼ 65 74½ 63½ Valdivia J Jr LB117 10.70 84-13 SwtRturn118no Byux1161½ Bould'Or1151¼ Btwn 2nd turn,n
6Jan07-3SA fm 1 Ⓣ:24 :48 1:111 1:352 4↑Alw 71256N$MY 98 6 64½ 64 64¼ 42 2¾ Valdivia J Jr LB118 5.40 86-13 Cervelo118¾ Tostd118¾ RunningFr118hd Came out str,will
20May06-5Hol fm 1⅛Ⓣ:47 1:10 1:342 1:46 + 4↑Alw 62800N$MY 91 6 53¾ 56 55 42¼ 45½ Flores D R LB119 3.90 95-08 Hndrx119nk FourtyNnrsSon1233 *Bcrx* 1172¼ 5wd into lane,n

WORKS: Nov12 Hol 4f fst :493 H *41/48* Nov5 Hol 5f fst 1:024 H *40/43* Oct29 Hol 3f fst :354 H *2/22* Oct22 Hol 4f fst :492 H *27/42* ●Sep29 Hol 6f fst 1:122 H *1/18* Sep22 Hol 6f fst 1:133 H *6/21*

TRAINER: Turf (172 .20 $2.41) Routes (314 .22 $2.34) Alw (59 .19 $2.38) J/T 2006-07 HOL (10 .40 $3.12) J/T 2006-07(34 .2

WORKOUT LINE

●	=	Best of day/distance
B	=	Breezing
D	=	Driving
(d)	=	Worked around dogs
E	=	Easily
g	=	Worked from gate
H	=	Handily
tr.t	=	Training track
TR	=	Training race
3/25	=	Workout ranking
(W)	=	Wood Chips
◇A	=	All weather track

from the starting gate, and "(d)," which shows the workout was around temporary cones ("dogs") placed out into the track to protect the inside paths. Times for these works are generally slower than other times at the same distance.

The attempt to interpret a Thoroughbred's workout regimen and bring some usefulness to the morning clocker's comments and recordings can be one of the trickiest handicapping factors at all class levels of racing. The main problem with analyzing workouts is that the average bettor just doesn't know what the trainer's overall intent is during the morning exercise, and also what physical conditions might be concealed through medications and treatment. Whether the horse is a cheap claimer or a Grade 1 stakes runner, sometimes injuries, lameness, soreness, and behavioral problems do occur. A good trainer will spot those problems and work to overcome them via rest, therapy, or even workouts. With maidens or juvenile runners, the problem isn't as complicated, because a long set of progressive workouts usually indicates a maiden that is being prepared with a solid foundation. The actual times of the maiden's works don't matter as much as his or her steady progression in time for race day.

For example, let's take a look at a New York-bred 2-year-old filly maiden special weight race from late fall of 2007 at Aqueduct racetrack, scheduled for one mile over the turf. In this event we can easily see two different ranges of basic juvenile workout preparation, eliminating any intricate trainer habits, patterns, or intentions.

Island Rose	Dk. b or br f. 2 (May)		Life	0 M 0 0	$0	-	D.Fst	0 0 0 0	$0	-
Own: Chin, Peter, A.	Sire: Strategic Mission (Mr. Prospector) $10,000		2007	0 M 0 0	$0	-	Wet (368*)	0 0 0 0	$0	-
Yellow, White Ball, Red Emblem, Red	Dam: Spruce Goose (Pine Bluff)		2006	0 M 0 0	$0	-	Turf (303)	0 0 0 0	$0	-
ards G G (-) 2007:(22 0 .00)	Br: Peter Kazamias(NY) 120		Aqu ⑦	0 0 0 0	$0	-	Dist (423)	0 0 0 0	$0	-
	Tr: Chin Peter (-) 2007:(25 0 .00)									

KS: Nov25 Bel tr.t 4f fst :50 Hg 38/72 Nov18 Bel tr.t 3f fst :391 B 26/28 Nov11 Bel 3f fst :38 B 2/3 Jun10 Aqu 3f fst :394 B 7/7

NER: 1stStart (3 .00 $0.00) 1stTurf (2 .00 $0.00) Turf (18 .00 $0.00) Routes (18 .00 $0.00) MdnSpWt (15 .00 $0.00)   J/T 2006-07 AQU (2 .00 $0.00) J/T 2006-07(8 .00 $0.00)

The workouts for Island Rose, trained by Peter Chin, only go four deep. They begin on June 10 with a three-furlong breeze in an unhurried 39⁴/5. Then, for some reason, there's an alarming five-month break before the next published three-furlong workout on November 11 at Belmont Park. This would be a classic example of a spotty and suspicious work tab, possibly indicating that there was an injury or illness that sidelined this filly and forced her into an extended summer vacation.

A more productive workout pattern, indicating fitness and reliability, is shown in the same event by number 6, Apocalyptical, and also by number 7, Donna Mira. These two fillies, trained by veterans Phil Serpe and Leah Gyarmati, show a combined 24 workouts between them leading up to today's event.

6	Apocalyptical	B. f.2 (Jan) FTKJUL06 $60,000	Life	0 M 0 0	$0	–	D.Fst	0 0 0 0
	Own: Flying Zee Stables	Sire: Wiseman's Ferry (Hennessy) $8,500	2007	0 M 0 0	$0	–	Wet (301*)	0 0 0 0
	Light Blue, White Yoke and 'ZZ,' White	Dam: Apocalyptic (Hickman Creek)	2006	0 M 0 0	$0	–	Turf (246*)	0 0 0 0
	Hill C (–) 2007:(1066 95 .09)	Br: Castellare di Cracchiolo Stables LLC(NY)	● 120					
		Tr: Serpe Philip M (–) 2007:(115 22 .19)	Aqu ⊕	0 0 0 0	$0	–	Dist (308*)	0 0 0 0

WORKS: Nov20 Bel tr.t 4f fst :49³ B 26/47 Nov8 Bel 5f fst 1:02⁴ B 16/25 Oct31 Bel tr.t 4f fst :50⁴ B 36/43 Oct6 Bel tr.t 4f fst :50¹ Bg 26/35 Sep30 Bel tr.t 5f fst 1:03³ B 19/25 Sep23 Bel tr.t 5f fst 1:03⁴ B 9/11
Sep16 Bel tr.t 4f fst :52¹ B 43/46 Sep9 Bel tr.t 4f fst :52 B 41/45 Aug27 Sar ⊕ tr.t 4f fm :48² H 20/36 Aug9 Sar 4f fst :51 B 76/79 Jly14 Bel tr.t 3f fst :36² B 6/18 Jly2 Bel tr.t 3f fst :37² B 6/11
TRAINER: 1stStart (26 .04 $0.44) 1stTurf (19 .05 $1.05) 2YO (24 .04 $0.29) Turf (149 .12 $1.17) Routes (181 .12 $1.29) MdnSpWt (88 .07 $0.73) J/T 2006-07 AQU (4 .25 $1.73) J/T 2006-07 (14 .07

7	Donna Mira	Dk. b or br f.2 (Mar)	Life	0 M 0 0	$0	–	D.Fst	0 0 0 0
	Own: Ferrari, Louis, P.	Sire: Diesis*GB (Sharpen Up*GB) $30,000	2007	0 M 0 0	$0	–	Wet (274)	0 0 0 0
	Blue and Red Diamonds, Blue Sleeves,	Dam: Silverwin (Silver Deputy)	2006	0 M 0 0	$0	–	Turf (325)	0 0 0 0
	Bridgmohan J V (–) 2007:(557 91 .16)	Br: Louis P. Ferrari(NY)	115⁵					
		Tr: Gyarmati Leah (–) 2007:(215 18 .08)	Aqu ⊕	0 0 0 0	$0	–	Dist (341)	0 0 0 0

WORKS: Nov24 Bel tr.t 4f fst :50⁴ B 71/89 Nov18 Bel tr.t 5f fst 1:04² B 33/36 Nov12 Bel tr.t 5f fst 1:03⁴ B 37/45 Nov5 Bel tr.t 4f fst :50³ B 67/84 Oct31 Bel tr.t 4f fst :51 B 38/43 Oct22 Bel 3f fst :36³ H 5/14
Oct14 Bel tr.t 4f fst :51¹ B 66/78 Sep30 Bel 3f fst :38 B 5/7 Sep16 Bel 4f fst :51² B 75/76 Sep9 Bel 4f fst :50 Bg 31/37 Aug26 Bel tr.t 5f fst 1:05⁴ B 25/25 Aug19 Bel tr.t 5f fst 1:06² B 21/21
TRAINER: 1stStart (20 .10 $6.28) 1stTurf (19 .00 $0.00) 2YO (36 .08 $1.43) Turf (70 .03 $0.37) Routes (175 .09 $1.08) MdnSpWt (75 .15 $3.15)

Fortunately, when dealing with a crop of older and more developed 3-year-olds preparing for the Kentucky Derby, we have more of a hardened workout pattern and foundation on which we can build some solid handicapping decisions. The workout reports provided in the weeks before the Kentucky Derby offer a wealth of information and should be observed carefully. *Daily Racing Form's* own Florida-based handicapper, Mike Welsch, provides an informative and descriptive column devoted to morning works leading up to the running of the Derby.

Although many horses have worked very well and then flopped in the afternoon, there's still a great deal of accuracy tied to some recent Derby winners and some also-rans that filled out the exotics. Take a look at some of Welsch's published pre-Derby workout notes from the last few years.

Street Sense: *The Barbaro of this year's Derby field as far as his morning work has gone, especially during a pair of works which couldn't have been more perfect. Finished up in 22 and change in both drills without need of urging and was equally impressive in his gallop-outs, during which he just kept going and going while clinging tight to the inside fence. Loves this track. The one to beat.*

Hard Spun: *Was just out for a routine gallop under trainer Larry Jones and he made by far the most favorable impression. He's an extremely attractive horse with good substance and a smooth, powerful look. He also looked extremely "happy" to me, as silly as that may sound. Or better put: He's a horse with a ton of quality and he couldn't be doing any better. He's looking more and more appealing, especially at expected odds of around 10–1.*

Work of the Day

*If Dick Vitale were on hand during training hours here Saturday, he would have described **Barbaro's** final Derby work (five furlongs in 59.48 seconds) as "Awesome, baby!"*

***Barbaro** and exercise rider Peter Brette had to call an audible just prior to beginning the work when a siren signaling a loose horse forced them to stop briefly as they approached the half-mile pole. Brette wisely waited until all was clear, backed **Barbaro** up an eighth of a mile, then turned around and began again.*

***Barbaro** broke off slowly, covering his opening eighth of a mile in 13.06 seconds and quarter in 25.06 before really leveling out and accelerating once entering the stretch. **Barbaro** proceeded to cover the next three furlongs in an eye-catching 34.42 around the turn to the seven-eighths pole before galloping out six furlongs in 1:12.14 with Brette offering little encouragement. In fact, he went so easily after crossing the finish line that it was difficult to tell when the actual work had ended and the gallop-out began. Track clockers credited him with a half-mile in 46 from the three-eighths to seven-eighths pole.*

*As noted Friday, **Barbaro** has the high leg action of a turf horse and as a result he does hit the ground harder than most. But the manner in which he stretches out effortlessly and covers ground more than makes up for his action, and **Barbaro** couldn't be doing any better coming into the Derby.*

Funny Cide: *One of the mystery horses having arrived on the scene late Wednesday. Did look well on the track Thursday morning and reportedly turned in a sensational five-furlong work at Belmont earlier this week. Finished just behind Empire Maker in the Wood. A definite factor.*

Empire Maker: *Until coming down with a minor foot bruise on Tuesday it was hard to find fault with the Derby favorite, whose gallops have* *been strong and his final work extremely impressive—a six-furlong drill completed around the turn in 1:12.72 in which he outfinished his stakes-winning stablemate Requete while seemingly doing little more than open galloping. Obviously the foot problem has hung a cloud over his head although if anything will likely elevate his final price . . . he's still the one to beat.*

Although it's always an encouraging sign to see your preferred horse work quickly, confidently, and comfortably over the surface he's scheduled to run on, it's even more important to locate horses that are having difficulty handling the surface and are uncomfortable with their surroundings. In these circumstances you might be able to eliminate a highly touted favorite or second choice whose previous successes were achieved elsewhere. Over the years, many horses have failed to handle the Churchill Downs surface for one reason or another, and there is no reason to believe that this will not continue to happen—especially with more and more synthetic racing surfaces being installed across the country.

Although arriving on the scene early in Louisville and working over the track is important, it is not entirely necessary, as shown by 2003 winner Funny Cide and 2005 longshot Giacomo. Both of these overlooked runners had no prior experience on the Churchill surface, but adjusted without a hitch. This is not the norm, however, as statistics have shown that *over 90 percent of the past Derby winners during the last 30 years have had appearances on the Churchill work tab prior to the event.* During the past couple of decades, several Derby winners have announced their sharp form and liking for the surface by working well at Churchill. However, it's also important to keep in mind that many of them would not have won without good trips, and several also-rans trained brilliantly over the track but were undone by poor racing luck.

On one hand, you don't want to spend too much time worrying about workouts, because you can never know for sure how much effort is being given in a specific drill. On the other hand, about two-thirds of Derby winners have a bullet work somewhere on their record, and almost three-quarters of horses have a fast breeze close to the Derby. That means that you pretty much have to look at workouts, but you don't want to get bogged down by them.

Street Sense, who won the 2006 Breeders' Cup Juvenile at Churchill Downs and then became the first Juvenile winner ever to win the Kentucky Derby, could easily be nominated as the poster child for the necessity of having workouts over Churchill. If his victory over the track in the Breeders' Cup seven months earlier were not enough proof, the last three out of four workouts leading up to the Derby were both sharp and encouraging. They were all indications that the son of Street Cry was not only fit, but also had a strong affinity for the Churchill Downs racing surface.

Derby Winner	Workout Date	Distance/Track Condition/Time
Street Sense	May 1	CD 5F fst 1:01 B 5/22
	April 24	•CD 5F fst :59 B 1/36
	April 10	CD 5F fst 1:04 B 38/39
	April 4	•CD 5F fst :58^2 B 1/6

Let's take a look at the statistical history from 1987 through 2006 and see what other Derby winners had sufficient workouts over the Churchill Downs surface. There are likely to be some favorable workout patterns that have developed.

Derby Winner	Workout Date	Distance/Track Condition/Time
Barbaro	April 29	•CD 4F fst :46 B 1/69
Giacomo	NO CHURCHILL DOWNS WORKS	
Smarty Jones	April 24	•CD 5F gd :58 B 1/34
Funny Cide	NO CHURCHILL DOWNS WORKS	
War Emblem	April 30	CD 5F fst 1:00^2 B 6/33
	April 24	•CD 6F fst 1:12^2 H 1/7
	April 18	CD 5F fst :59^3 B 3/21
Monarchos	April 27	CD 4F fst :48^4 B 6/26
	April 8	CD 5F fst 1:00^1 B 4/22
	April 1	CD 5F sly 1:02^2 B 3/10
Fusaichi Pegasus	April 30	CD 6F fst 1:14^3 B 3/6
Charismatic	April 26	CD 5F sly 1:02^4 B 11/26
	April 11	CD 4F fst :50 B 11/18

Derby Winner	Workout Date	Distance/Track Condition/Time
Real Quiet	April 28	•CD 5F fst :59^1 H 1/29
	April 23	CD 6F fst 1:12^2 H 2/6
	April 18	•CD 5F fst 1:00^1 H 1/52
Silver Charm	April 29	•CD 5F fst 1:00^3 B 1/35
	April 24	•CD 6F fst 1:13 H 1/8
	April 19	•CD 5F my 1:00^2 H 1/27
Grindstone	April 27	•CD 6F fst 1:14 B 1/15
	April 22	CD 4F fst :50 B 14/37
	April 6	CD 5F fst 1:01 B 2/28
	March 29	CD 6F sly 1:13^3 H 1/2
Thunder Gulch	May 1	CD 5F fst 1:00^2 H 3/27
	April 24	•CD 6F sly 1:14 H 1/7
Go for Gin	May 1	CD 6F gd 1:15 H 2/3
	April 25	CD 5F fst 1:04^3 H 27/32
Sea Hero	April 29	CD 3F fst :36^3 B
	April 23	•CD 6F fst 1:14^2 H
Lil E. Tee	April 29	CD 4F fst :48 B
Strike the Gold	May 1	CD 4F fst :51^2 B
	April 26	•CD 5F fst 1:00 H
	April 21	CD 5F fst 1:05 B
Unbridled	May 1	CD 5F fst 1:01^4 B
	April 25	•CD 6F fst 1:13 H
Sunday Silence	May 4	•CD 4F fst :46^3 H
	April 29	•CD 8F sly 1:39^3 H
	April 24	CD 7F fst 1:28 H
Winning Colors	May 3	CD 4F fst :49 B
	April 26	CD 6F fst 1:13^1 B
Alysheba	April 30	CD 4F fst :47 H

If we add Street Sense from 2007 and break down these Churchill Down workouts over the last 21 runnings, we can uncover some patterns that are worth noting:

- 19 of the last 21 winners (90 percent) had at least one workout over Churchill Downs.
- 13 of the last 21 winners (62 percent) posted one or more bullet workouts at Churchill Downs.
- 14 of the last 21 winners (66 percent) had two or more workouts at Churchill Downs.
- 9 of the last 21 winners (43 percent) show a workout within one week of race day.

DERBY PREPS:
PATHS TO GLORY

WHEN FACED WITH the challenge of trying to foresee which one of 20 or so unpredictable, still-maturing 3-year-olds will win the Kentucky Derby, some horseplayers look to historical trends and statistics for guidance. Just when you think you have a set of handicapping rules for soundly and confidently downgrading an entrant's chances, though, the rules are broken.

In recent years, several Derby winners have defied history. The rail-skimming victory by Street Sense in 2007 exploded several statistical maxims that handicappers had followed for decades, beginning with the fact that the colt became the first Breeders' Cup Juvenile winner to succeed in the Derby. Since 1984, the year of the inaugural Breeders' Cup, 13 winners of the Juvenile had entered the starting gate at Churchill Downs on the first Saturday in May, and all had failed to win the Derby. (The nine others didn't make it to Louisville.)

In addition, no horse had won the Derby with two preps or fewer as a 3-year-old since Sunny's Halo in 1983. Before that it was Jet Pilot in 1947. Street Sense also became the first 2-year-old champion to win the Kentucky Derby since Spectacular Bid in 1979.

In 2006, Barbaro bucked another historical trend by winning the

Derby off a five-week layoff. Prior to his victory, no horse had won the Kentucky Derby off a layoff of four weeks or more since Needles in 1956. In the days leading up to the 2006 Derby, there was no shortage of quotes and advice from Hall of Fame trainers who sermonized that a horse needed three prep races as a 3-year-old before running at Churchill. Barbaro romped to a 6½-length victory.

"Last year I was the most unorthodox trainer there was and now this year all these people look like geniuses because they're taking five, six, and seven weeks off between the races," said Barbaro's trainer, Michael Matz, in a *Daily Racing Form* interview before the 2007 running. "When I did it, it was voodoo."

Here are some other historical trends and tidbits to add to the complexity of handicapping the race.

- No horse since Apollo in 1882 has won the Kentucky Derby without having started as a 2-year-old, and no horse has won the Derby with four or fewer career starts since Exterminator in 1918.
- Since 1955, horses that have not started as 2-year-olds are 0 for 42 in the Derby, but in their defense, most were sent off at long odds.
- No horse since Morvich in 1922 has won the Derby off a layoff of as long as eight weeks.
- No entrant in the last 61 years has won the Derby without having run a mile and an eighth.

Although there may be some reliability and helpfulness in these statistical trends, it's much more important to understand that streaks are meant to be broken.

Not so long ago, no responsible handicapper would have considered betting a Derby horse that had not had a strong foundation as a 2-year-old and several solid preps at 3. They say the game is very different now, however, and many people believe that a fresh, lightly raced horse is the most dangerous kind. That has proven to be the case in almost every other type of stakes race, so why not the Kentucky Derby too? Even the Breeders' Cup races have been won in recent years by horses that have come into the event off significant layoffs. The truth is, there is no single factor that should eliminate a contender from consideration.

That said, have historical trends and statistical norms become irrelevant in this new and very different era of horse racing, or do they still matter in the Kentucky Derby? I believe the answer to the second half of that question is a resounding yes.

THE JUVENILE JINX AND DERBY PREP RACES

ONE HANDICAPPING PRINCIPLE that has stood the test of time is the reliability and importance of a Derby hopeful having an encouraging race in his or her final prep. Basically, that means you want to see an in-the-money or close fourth-place finish.

By no means is this an earth-shattering angle, and most entrants every year will meet that standard. It is worthwhile to note, though, that every Derby winner in the last 50 years has had what would qualify as a "sharp" race leading up to the big event.

Another reliable method is to evaluate the quality of the traditional prep races leading up to the Kentucky Derby. It's no secret that the Derby winner can come from almost anywhere. Although most are Kentucky-breds, there have also been success stories from such unlikely locales as Montana, Missouri, and Tennessee. The winning colt or filly could be the product of superior bloodlines, trained and developed on the wealthiest breeding farm and guided by the industry's top connections, like 2000 winner Fusaichi Pegasus, purchased for $4 million; on the flip side, he or she might have been a $17,500 bargain like Seattle Slew, the offspring of an unproven or unfashionable stallion, hand-picked and developed by a low-profile owner or trainer.

Despite the wide variety in the quality and handling of Derby hopefuls, one thing that remains consistent is the geographical path they take on the road to Louisville. A careful sampling of the last 20 years reveals that many past winners had significant 3-year-old prep races in New York, Florida, Southern California, Kentucky, Louisiana, and Arkansas. In fact, it's interesting to note that War Emblem, acquired by Prince Ahmed bin Salman's Thoroughbred Corporation and sent to trainer Bob Baffert after his 2002 Illinois Derby romp, was the only horse in the last two decades who did not have a traditional prep race in one of the states that typically produce the Derby winner. Let's take a look.

Year	Winner	Last Prep Race	Next-to-Last Prep Race
2007	Street Sense	G1 Blue Grass (Ky.)	G3 Tampa Bay Derby (Fl.)
2006	Barbaro	G1 Florida Derby (Fl.)	G3 Holy Bull (Fl.)
2005	Giacomo	G1 Santa Anita Derby (Ca.)	G2 San Felipe (Ca.)
2004	Smarty Jones	G2 Arkansas Derby (Ark.)	Rebel Stakes (Ark.)
2003	Funny Cide	G1 Wood Memorial (NY)	G2 Louisiana Derby (La.)
2002	War Emblem	G2 Illinois Derby (Ill.)	Allowance Race (Ill.)
2001	Monarchos	G1 Wood Memorial (NY)	G1 Florida Derby (Fl.)
2000	Fusaichi Pegasus	G1 Wood Memorial (NY)	G2 San Felipe (Ca.)
1999	Charismatic	G2 Lexington (Ky.)	G1 Santa Anita Derby (Ca.)
1998	Real Quiet	G1 Santa Anita Derby (Ca.)	G2 San Felipe (Ca.)
1997	Silver Charm	G1 Santa Anita Derby (Ca.)	G2 San Felipe (Ca.)
1996	Grindstone	G2 Arkansas Derby (Ark.)	G3 Louisiana Derby (La.)
1995	Thunder Gulch	G2 Blue Grass (Ky.)	G1 Florida Derby (Fl.)
1994	Go for Gin	G1 Wood Memorial (NY)	G1 Florida Derby (Fl.)
1993	Sea Hero	G2 Blue Grass (Ky.)	Allowance Race (Fl.)
1992	Lil E. Tee	G2 Arkansas Derby (Ark.)	G2 Jim Beam (Ky.)
1991	Strike the Gold	G2 Blue Grass (Ky.)	G1 Florida Derby (Fl.)
1990	Unbridled	G2 Blue Grass (Ky.)	G1 Florida Derby (Fl.)
1989	Sunday Silence	G1 Santa Anita Derby (Ca.)	G2 San Felipe (Ca.)
1988	Winning Colors	G1 Santa Anita Derby (Ca.)	G1 Santa Anita Oaks (Ca.)

Is there one final prep race that has dominated over the past 20 years? The answer is no. There has been a fairly equal distribution among the four major prep races. The Santa Anita Derby (5 wins), Blue Grass Stakes (5), Wood Memorial (4), and Arkansas Derby (3) make up 85 percent of the prep races that have produced a Derby winner. This is a significant finding and a good barometer as to where your next Derby winner is likely to come from, not only this year, but also in the foreseeable future. In the overall history of Derby prep races, the Blue Grass (23), Wood Memorial (19), and Florida Derby (18) are still the "big three."

ARKANSAS DERBY (3)

Year	Horse	Finish
1996	Grindstone	2nd
1992	Lil E. Tee	2nd
1983	Sunny's Halo	1st

BLUE GRASS (23)

Year	Horse	Finish
2007	Street Sense	2nd
1995	Thunder Gulch	4th
1993	Sea Hero	4th
1991	Strike the Gold	1st
1990	Unbridled	3rd
1987	Alysheba	3rd
1979	Spectacular Bid	1st
1972	Riva Ridge	1st
1970	Dust Commander	1st
1968	Forward Pass	1st
1967	Proud Clarion	2nd
1965	Lucky Debonair	1st
1964	Northern Dancer	1st
1963	Chateaugay	1st
1962	Decidedly	2nd
1959	Tomy Lee	1st
1942	Shut Out	1st
1941	Whirlaway	2nd
1926	Bubbling Over	1st
1921	Behave Yourself	2nd
1913	Donerail	2nd
1911	Meridian	2nd
1903	Judge Himes	3rd

FLAMINGO (13)

Year	Horse	Finish
1979	Spectacular Bid	1st
1977	Seattle Slew	1st
1975	Foolish Pleasure	1st
1974	Cannonade	7th
1968	Forward Pass	4th

Year	Horse	Finish
1964	Northern Dancer	1st
1961	Carry Back	1st
1958	Tim Tam	1st
1957	Iron Liege	3rd
1956	Needles	1st
1951	Count Turf	6th
1948	Citation	1st
1938	Lawrin	1st

FLORIDA DERBY (18)

Year	Horse	Finish
1995	Thunder Gulch	1st
1994	Go for Gin	4th
1991	Strike the Gold	2nd
1990	Unbridled	1st
1984	Swale	1st
1981	Pleasant Colony	5th
1979	Spectacular Bid	1st
1975	Foolish Pleasure	3rd
1974	Cannonade	2nd
1968	Forward Pass	1st
1966	Kauai King	5th
1964	Northern Dancer	1st
1961	Carry Back	1st
1960	Venetian Way	2nd
1958	Tim Tam	1st
1957	Iron Liege	3rd
1956	Needles	1st
1953	Dark Star	13th

FOUNTAIN OF YOUTH (10)

Year	Horse	Finish
1995	Thunder Gulch	1st
1994	Go for Gin	2nd
1990	Unbridled	3rd
1984	Swale	3rd
1981	Pleasant Colony	2nd
1979	Spectacular Bid	1st

Year	Horse	Finish
1968	Forward Pass	4th
1966	Kauai King	1st
1961	Carry Back	3rd
1958	Tim Tam	1st

GOTHAM (1)

Year	Horse	Finish
1973	Secretariat	1st

HUTCHESON (3)

Year	Horse	Finish
1984	Swale	1st
1979	Spectacular Bid	1st
1966	Kauai King	2nd

ILLINOIS DERBY (1)

Year	Horse	Finish
2002	War Emblem	1st

LEXINGTON (2)

Year	Horse	Finish
1999	Charismatic	1st
1984	Swale	2nd

LOUISIANA DERBY (3)

Year	Horse	Finish
2003	Funny Cide	3rd
1996	Grindstone	1st
1924	Black Gold	1st

REBEL (2)

Year	Horse	Finish
2004	Smarty Jones	1st
1983	Sunny's Halo	1st

SAN FELIPE (10)

Year	Horse	Finish
2000	Fusaichi Pegasus	1st

Year	Horse	Finish
1998	Real Quiet	2nd
1997	Silver Charm	2nd
1989	Sunday Silence	1st
1987	Alysheba	2nd
1978	Affirmed	1st
1965	Lucky Debonair	2nd
1959	Tomy Lee	2nd
1954	Determine	1st
1947	Jet Pilot	6th

SANTA ANITA DERBY (14)

Year	Horse	Finish
1999	Charismatic	4th
1998	Real Quiet	2nd
1997	Silver Charm	2nd
1989	Sunday Silence	1st
1988	Winning Colors	1st
1986	Ferdinand	3rd
1982	Gato del Sol	4th
1978	Affirmed	1st
1969	Majestic Prince	1st
1965	Lucky Debonair	1st
1955	Swaps	1st
1954	Determine	1st
1952	Hill Gail	1st
1940	Gallahadion	13th

SAN VICENTE (9)

Year	Horse	Finish
1997	Silver Charm	1st
1976	Bold Forbes	3rd
1969	Majestic Prince	1st
1965	Lucy Debonair	1st
1959	Tomy Lee	2nd
1955	Swaps	1st
1954	Determine	2nd
1952	Hill Gail	1st
1940	Gallahadion	1st

SPIRAL/JIM BEAM LANE'S END STAKES (1)

Year	Horse	Finish
1992	Lil E. Tee	1st

WOOD MEMORIAL (19)

Year	Horse	Finish
2003	Funny Cide	2nd
2000	Fusaichi Pegasus	1st
1994	Go for Gin	2nd
1981	Pleasant Colony	1st
1980	Genuine Risk	3rd
1977	Seattle Slew	1st
1976	Bold Forbes	1st
1975	Foolish Pleasure	1st
1973	Secretariat	3rd
1961	Carry Back	2nd
1951	Count Turf	5th
1950	Middleground	2nd
1946	Assault	1st
1945	Hoop Jr.	1st
1943	Count Fleet	1st
1939	Johnstown	1st
1935	Omaha	3rd
1931	Twenty Grand	1st
1930	Gallant Fox	1st

It's also interesting and valuable to look at past Derby winners' 2-year-old seasons to see if there are any trends or patterns that emerge among late-in-the-year stakes races. As mentioned earlier in the chapter, in 2007 Street Sense became the first Breeders' Cup Juvenile winner to take the Derby the next spring. Circular Quay, Great Hunter, Teuflesberg, Scat Daddy, and Stormello also ran in the 2006 Juvenile, but the best Derby performance among those five was a sixth-place finish by Circular Quay at 11–1.

FOURTH RACE
Churchill
NOVEMBER 4, 2006

$1\frac{1}{16}$ MILES. (1.41^{1}) 23RD RUNNING OF THE BESSEMER TRUST BREEDERS' CUP JUVENILE. Grade I. Purse $2,000,000 FOR COLTS AND GELDINGS, TWO YEARS OLD. Weight: 122 lbs.; $20,000 to pre-enter, $30,000 to enter, with guaranteed $2 million purse including nominator awards (plus Net Supplementary Fees, if any), of which 54% of all monies to the owner of the winner, 20% to second, 10% to third, 5.1% to fourth and 2.5% to fifth; plus stallion nominator awards of 2.7% of all monies to the winner, 1% to second and 0.5% to third and foal nominator awards of 2.7% of all monies to the winner, 1% to second and 0.5% to third.Closed with 15 pre-entries.

Value of Race: $1,832,000 Winner $1,080,000; second $400,000; third $200,000; fourth $102,000; fifth $50,000. Mutuel Pool $3,924,658.00 Exacta Pool $3,017,511.00 Trifecta Pool $2,505,374.00 Superfecta Pool $834,402.00

Last Raced	Horse	M/Eqt.	A.	Wt	PP	St	¼	½	¾	Str	Fin	Jockey	Odds $1
7Oct06 ^{8}Kee^{3}	Street Sense	L f	2	122	1	9	13^{2}	12^{hd}	9^{1}	1^{4}	1^{10}	Borel C H	15.20
7Oct06 ^{8}Kee^{2}	Circular Quay	L	2	122	9	14	14	14	7^{hd}	$3^{1\frac{1}{2}}$	$2^{2\frac{1}{4}}$	Gomez G K	3.00
7Oct06 ^{8}Kee^{1}	Great Hunter	L b	2	122	7	6	$9^{\frac{1}{2}}$	$9^{2\frac{1}{2}}$	5^{2}	2^{hd}	$3^{2\frac{3}{4}}$	Nakatani C S	7.00
14Oct06 ^{9}Bel^{1}	Scat Daddy	L	2	122	3	2	4^{hd}	$4^{\frac{1}{2}}$	3^{2}	5^{3}	$4^{\frac{3}{4}}$	Velazquez J R	3.70
8Oct06 ^{8}OSA^{1}	Stormello	L b	2	122	2	1	$2^{\frac{1}{2}}$	2^{hd}	$2^{\frac{1}{2}}$	4^{hd}	$5^{6\frac{1}{4}}$	Desormeaux K J	9.90
23Sep06 ^{9}Bel^{2}	C P West	L	2	122	5	12	8^{1}	8^{1}	$4^{1\frac{1}{2}}$	$6^{1\frac{1}{2}}$	$6^{6\frac{3}{4}}$	Bejarano R	10.20
30Sep06 ^{9}TP^{1}	U D Ghetto	L	2	122	12	10	$12^{1\frac{1}{2}}$	$13^{1\frac{1}{2}}$	14	$8^{\frac{1}{2}}$	$7^{9\frac{3}{4}}$	Smith M E	30.70
23Sep06 ^{9}Bel^{1}	King of the Roxy	L b	2	122	4	3	5^{hd}	7^{hd}	13^{3}	13^{8}	$8^{1\frac{1}{4}}$	Prado E S	17.50
9Oct06 ^{8}WO^{1}	Skip Code	L b	2	122	14	13	11^{1}	11^{4}	12^{hd}	$11^{2\frac{1}{2}}$	9^{hd}	Husbands P	60.80
22Oct06 ^{5}Kee^{1}	Teuflesberg	L b	2	122	8	11	10^{2}	10^{1}	10^{2}	$9^{\frac{1}{2}}$	$10^{2\frac{1}{4}}$	Albarado R J	78.40
14Oct06 ^{9}Bel^{3}	Pegasus Wind	L b	2	122	10	4	$3^{2\frac{1}{2}}$	3^{1}	1^{hd}	7^{6}	$11^{2\frac{3}{4}}$	Luzzi M J	10.30
8Oct06 ^{8}OSA^{6}	Malt Magic	L b	2	122	13	7	$7^{1\frac{1}{2}}$	6^{1}	6^{1}	10^{hd}	12^{9}	Court J K	53.40
14Oct06 ^{9}Bel^{5}	Got the Last Laugh	L	2	122	11	8	$6^{\frac{1}{2}}$	5^{hd}	8^{hd}	12^{2}	13	Douglas R R	65.80
8Oct06 ^{8}OSA^{2}	Principle Secret	L	2	122	6	5	1^{hd}	1^{hd}	11^{1}	14	—	Espinoza V	6.50

OFF AT 1:11 Start Good For All But U D GHETTO. Won driving. Track fast.

TIME :23, :46^{3}, 1:11^{3}, 1:36^{2}, 1:42^{2} (:23.07, :46.67, 1:11.74, 1:36.50, 1:42.59)

$2 Mutuel Prices:				
	1 – STREET SENSE	32.40	12.60	8.00
	9 – CIRCULAR QUAY		5.00	3.20
	7 – GREAT HUNTER			4.40

$2 EXACTA 1–9 PAID $181.20 $2 TRIFECTA 1–9–7 PAID $996.00
$2 SUPERFECTA 1–9–7–3 PAID $3,915.80

Dk. b or br. c, (Feb), by Street Cry-Ire – Bedazzle , by Dixieland Band . Trainer Nafzger Carl A. Bred by James Tafel (Ky).

TENTH RACE
Churchill
MAY 5, 2007

$1\frac{1}{4}$ MILES. (1.59^{2}) 133RD RUNNING OF THE KENTUCKY DERBY PRESENTED BY YUM! BRANDS. Grade I. Purse $2,000,000 FOR THREE-YEAR-OLDS WITH AN ENTRY FEE OF $25,000 EACH AND A STARTING FEE OF $25,000 EACH. The winner shall receive $1,240,000, second place $400,000, third $200,000, fourth $100,000 and fifth $60,000. The maximum number of runners shall be limited to twenty. Weight 126 lbs.

Value of Race: $2,210,000 Winner $1,450,000; second $400,000; third $200,000; fourth $100,000; fifth $60,000. Mutuel Pool $49,564,991.00 Exacta Pool $22,764,587.00 Trifecta Pool $27,601,096.00 Superfecta Pool $8,979,962.00

Last Raced	Horse	M/Eqt.	A.	Wt	PP	¼	½	¾	1	Str	Fin	Jockey	Odds $1
14Apr07 ^{9}Kee^{2}	Street Sense	L f	3	126	7	$18^{\frac{1}{2}}$	19^{5}	17^{hd}	3^{hd}	1^{1}	$1^{2\frac{1}{4}}$	Borel C H	4.90
24Mar07 ^{10}TP^{1}	Hard Spun	L	3	126	8	1^{hd}	1^{1}	1^{2}	1^{3}	2^{4}	$2^{5\frac{3}{4}}$	Pino M G	10.00
14Apr07 ^{11}OP^{1}	Curlin	L	3	126	2	$13^{\frac{1}{2}}$	$13^{2\frac{1}{2}}$	$14^{1\frac{1}{2}}$	8^{hd}	6^{1}	$3^{\frac{1}{2}}$	Albarado R J	5.00
31Mar07 ^{11}GP^{6}	Imawildandcrzyguy	L b	3	126	5	20	20	20	$16^{\frac{1}{2}}$	$11^{1\frac{1}{2}}$	$4^{\frac{1}{2}}$	Guidry M	28.90
6Apr07 ^{9}Kee^{4}	Sedgefield	L b	3	126	1	$5^{\frac{1}{2}}$	$5^{1\frac{1}{2}}$	3^{hd}	$2^{\frac{1}{2}}$	3^{hd}	5^{nk}	Leparoux J R	58.60
10Mar07 ^{9}FG^{1}	Circular Quay	L	3	126	16	19^{3}	18^{1}	16^{hd}	$13^{\frac{1}{2}}$	$8^{\frac{1}{2}}$	$6^{\frac{3}{4}}$	Velazquez J R	11.40
7Apr07 ^{6}SA^{1}	Tiago	L	3	126	15	17^{hd}	$17^{\frac{1}{2}}$	18^{4}	15^{1}	12^{hd}	$7^{\frac{1}{2}}$	Smith M E	14.80
7Apr07 ^{8}Aqu^{3}	Any Given Saturday	L	3	126	18	$8^{\frac{1}{2}}$	$9^{1\frac{1}{2}}$	9^{1}	4^{hd}	$4^{2\frac{1}{2}}$	$8^{2\frac{1}{2}}$	Gomez G K	13.60
7Apr07 ^{6}SA^{3}	Sam P.	L	3	126	13	$12^{2\frac{1}{2}}$	$12^{1\frac{1}{2}}$	$12^{1\frac{1}{2}}$	7^{hd}	$7^{1\frac{1}{2}}$	$9^{1\frac{3}{4}}$	Dominguez R A	43.70
7Apr07 ^{8}Aqu^{1}	Nobiz Like Shobiz	L b	3	126	12	6^{hd}	$6^{1\frac{1}{2}}$	6^{1}	5^{hd}	5^{hd}	10^{3}	Velasquez C	10.40
14Apr07 ^{9}Kee^{1}	Dominican	L	3	126	19	$11^{1\frac{1}{2}}$	10^{hd}	10^{hd}	$10^{\frac{1}{2}}$	$14^{2\frac{1}{2}}$	11^{nk}	Bejarano R	24.90
14Apr07 ^{9}Kee^{3}	Zanjero	L	3	126	3	16^{2}	15^{3}	13^{hd}	$11^{\frac{1}{2}}$	$10^{\frac{1}{2}}$	$12^{2\frac{3}{4}}$	Bridgmohan S X	36.00
14Apr07 ^{9}Kee^{5}	Great Hunter	L b	3	126	20	$9^{\frac{1}{2}}$	$11^{2\frac{1}{2}}$	$11^{1\frac{1}{2}}$	$6^{\frac{1}{2}}$	9^{hd}	$13^{1\frac{3}{4}}$	Nakatani C S	25.30
7Apr07 ^{6}SA^{4}	Liquidity	L	3	126	9	$10^{\frac{1}{2}}$	$8^{\frac{1}{2}}$	$7^{\frac{1}{2}}$	9^{hd}	13^{1}	$14^{\frac{3}{4}}$	Flores D R	40.00
7Apr07 ^{6}SA^{5}	Bwana Bull	L b	3	126	11	14^{2}	14^{hd}	15^{1}	$19^{\frac{1}{2}}$	16^{2}	15^{1}	Castellano J J	50.30
14Apr07 ^{11}OP^{2}	Storm in May	L	3	126	4	$15^{1\frac{1}{2}}$	16^{hd}	$19^{2\frac{1}{2}}$	18^{2}	$15^{\frac{1}{2}}$	$16^{11\frac{1}{2}}$	Leyva J C	27.20
14Apr07 ^{9}Kee^{4}	Teuflesberg	L	3	126	10	4^{1}	$3^{\frac{1}{2}}$	$2^{\frac{1}{2}}$	12^{hd}	$17^{\frac{1}{2}}$	$17^{2\frac{3}{4}}$	Elliott S	51.90
31Mar07 ^{11}GP^{1}	Scat Daddy	L	3	126	14	7^{1}	7^{hd}	8^{hd}	20	20	$18^{6\frac{1}{4}}$	Prado E S	7.20
31Mar07 ^{11}GP^{4}	Stormello	L b	3	126	17	2^{hd}	4^{1}	5^{hd}	$14^{1\frac{1}{2}}$	$18^{1\frac{1}{2}}$	$19^{7\frac{1}{4}}$	Desormeaux K J	44.80
7Apr07 ^{7}Haw^{1}	Cowtown Cat	L	3	126	6	$3^{\frac{1}{2}}$	$2^{\frac{1}{2}}$	4^{1}	$17^{1\frac{1}{2}}$	$19^{\frac{1}{2}}$	20	Jara F	19.80

OFF AT 6:16 Start Good. Won driving. Track fast.

TIME :22^{4}, :46^{1}, 1:11, 1:37, 2:02 (:22.96, :46.26, 1:11.13, 1:37.04, 2:02.17)

$2 Mutuel Prices:

7 – STREET SENSE	11.80	6.40	4.60
8 – HARD SPUN		9.80	7.00
2 – CURLIN			5.60

$2 EXACTA 7–8 PAID $101.80 $2 TRIFECTA 7–8–2 PAID $440.00
$2 SUPERFECTA 7–8–2–5 PAID $29,046.40

Dk. b or br. c, (Feb), by Street Cry-Ire – Bedazzle , by Dixieland Band . Trainer Nafzger Carl A. Bred by James Tafel (Ky).

Below is a rundown of Breeders' Cup Juvenile participants who ran in the Derby the next year, arranged by their order of finish at Churchill. A total of 62 horses have attempted the Breeders' Cup Juvenile/Kentucky Derby sweep, but only Street Sense has been successful in both races.

Year	Horse	BC Juv. Finish	Derby Finish
2006	Street Sense	1st	1st
	Circular Quay	2nd	6th
	Great Hunter	3rd	13th
	Teuflesberg	10th	17th
	Scat Daddy	4th	18th
	Stormello	5th	19th
2005	Brother Derek	4th	4th
	Private Vow	14th	15th
2004	Afleet Alex	2nd	3rd
	Wilko	1st	6th
	Sun King	3rd	15th
2003	Action This Day	1st	6th
	Minister Eric	2nd	16th
2002	Lone Star Sky	11th	15th
2001	Came Home	7th	6th
	Johannesburg	1st	8th
	Essence of Dubai	12th	9th
	Saarland	8th	10th
2000	Point Given	2nd	5th
	A P Valentine	7th	7th
	Dollar Bill	10th	15th
1999	Captain Steve	11th	8th
	Anees	1st	13th
	High Yield	3rd	15th
	Graeme Hall	12th	19th
1998	Cat Thief	3rd	3rd
	Lemon Drop Kid	5th	9th
	Answer Lively	1st	10th
1997	Favorite Trick	1st	8th
	Nationalore	3rd	9th

Year	Horse	BC Juv. Finish	Derby Finish
1996	*NONE		
1995	Unbridled's Song	1st	5th
	Editor's Note	3rd	6th
	Diligence	5th	9th
	Honour and Glory	4th	18th
1994	Tejano Run	3rd	2nd
	Timber Country	1st	3rd
	Eltish	2nd	6th
	Talkin Man	10th	12th
1993	Blumin Affair	2nd	3rd
	Brocco	1st	4th
	Tabasco Cat	3rd	6th
1992	Sea Hero	7th	1st
1991	Dance Floor	6th	3rd
	Pine Bluff	5th	5th
	Arazi	1st	8th
	Snappy Landing	3rd	17th
1990	Best Pal	6th	2nd
	Fly So Free	1st	5th
	Happy Jazz Band	4th	11th
1989	Pleasant Tap	6th	3rd
1988	Easy Goer	2nd	2nd
1987	Regal Classic	2nd	5th
1986	Alysheba	3rd	1st
	Bet Twice	4th	2nd
	Gulch	5th	6th
	Capote	1st	DNF
	Demons Begone	6th	DNF
1985	Mogambo	6th	10th
	Groovy	10th	16th
1984	Spend a Buck	3rd	1st
	Chief's Crown	1st	3rd
	Tank's Prospect	2nd	7th

Although the Grade 1 Hollywood Futurity has produced the most winners from key 2-year-old prep paths in the last two decades, it has become the norm for trainers to take a more conservative approach regarding how they handle their talented juveniles. More and more trainers are giving these youngsters only one to three races and are skipping many of the big 2-year-old stakes in an attempt to leave more in the tank for the 3-year-old season. As the following list clearly indicates, there are no distinct 2-year-old prep-race patterns worth investigating in attempting to sift out a Derby winner for the next year.

Year	Winner	Last 2-Year-Old Race	Next-to-Last 2-Year-old Race
2007	Street Sense	G1 Breeders' Cup Juvenile (Ky.)	G1 Breeders' Futurity (Ky.)
2006	Barbaro	Laurel Futurity (Md.)	Maiden Special Weight (Del.)
2005	Giacomo	G1 Hollywood Futurity (Ca.)	Allowance (Ca.)
2004	Smarty Jones	Penn Nursery Stakes (Pa.)	Maiden Special Weight (Pa.)
2003	Funny Cide	Sleepy Hollow Stakes (NY)	B.F. Bongard Stakes (NY)
2002	War Emblem	Allowance (La.)	Manila Stakes (Ill.)
2001	Monarchos	Maiden Special Weight (Ky.)	Maiden Special Weight (Ky.)
2000	Fusaichi Pegasus	Maiden Special Weight (Ca.)	
1999	Charismatic	Allowance (Ca.)	Maiden Claiming $62,500 (Ca.)
1998	Real Quiet	G1 Hollywood Futurity (Ca.)	G3 B & W Ky. JC (Ky.)
1997	Silver Charm	G2 Del Mar Futurity (Ca.)	Maiden Special Weight (Ca.)
1996	Grindstone	G3 Bashford Manor (Ky.)	Maiden Special Weight (NY)
1995	Thunder Gulch	G1 Hollywood Futurity (Ca.)	G2 Remsen (NY)
1994	Go for Gin	G2 Remsen (NY)	Chief's Crown (NY)
1993	Sea Hero	G1 Breeders' Cup Juvenile (Ky.)	G1 Champagne (NY)
1992	Lil E. Tee	Allowance (Ky.)	Allowance (Ky.)
1991	Strike the Gold	Maiden Special Weight (NY)	Maiden Special Weight (NY)
1990	Unbridled	What a Pleasure (Fl.)	In Reality (Fl.)
1989	Sunday Silence	Allowance (Ca.)	Maiden Special Weight (Ca.)
1988	Winning Colors	Allowance (Ca.)	Maiden Special Weight (NY)

7

BIG-DAY JOCKEYS AND TRAINERS

IN 1892, THE KENTUCKY DERBY was in its 18th year. That was three more years than the winning jockey, Alonzo "Lonnie" Clayton, had been alive. At 15, Clayton was, and remains, the youngest winning rider in Derby history. At the other end of the spectrum, Bill Shoemaker became the oldest jockey to win the race when he brought Ferdinand home at odds of nearly 18–1 in 1986.

No matter how old the jockey, riding in the Kentucky Derby probably carries more pressure than any event in Thoroughbred racing. How the participants respond to that pressure—especially those experiencing it for the first time—usually goes a long way toward deciding which horse or horses will hit the board on the first Saturday in May.

Generally speaking, you don't want to pick a horse with a trainer or jockey that's making his or her first trip to the Derby. There's no telling how an inexperienced jockey will react when he hears the strains of *My Old Kentucky Home* on that special late Saturday afternoon. Not every rider has the coolness and talent of 18-year-old Steve Cauthen, who piloted Affirmed to victory in 1978 and later became the youngest rider to sweep the Triple Crown.

In addition, the stress of the media blitz leading up to the event is overwhelming, and inexperienced connections are far more likely to make tactical errors during the weeks of preparation and the eventual race-day ride.

It's also important to select a horse that has a familiar pilot on board. A jockey really needs to know his or her horse in a race as taxing as the Derby, where one poor decision could leave the pair hung out 10-wide on the first turn and hopelessly beaten before the real running even begins. You might be able to make exceptions to this rule for some of the top jockeys, but many handicappers still regard it as a negative factor when even a seasoned veteran takes the irons for the very first time.

Multiple Derby-winning trainers D. Wayne Lukas (who holds the record for total starters in the race, with 42) and Bob Baffert know a thing or two about how important experience is on the big day. They recently had these public thoughts on the significance of preparation and seasoning

"The experience factor is paramount," said Lukas, who has trained four Derby winners. "Every young trainer who runs a horse in the Derby for the first or second time walks away a lot smarter because of it."

According to Baffert, experience is always a major factor when he seeks a rider for his Derby starters.

"I want to go in the Derby with a rider who has ridden the race before. I think it's very important," he said. "After last year, I said to my wife that I would never bring a rider here for the first time again. It's overwhelming for them."

Trainer statistics are highly constructive handicapping tools, particularly in relation to the biggest race in America. Familiarizing yourself with the strengths and weaknesses of the people behind and aboard your Derby selection is crucial. Although the ability of the jockey is extremely important, most of his or her success depends upon the ability of the horse and the competence of the trainer.

The trainer's statistics are shown at the bottom of each horse's past-performance lines in *Daily Racing Form*. These stats reveal the trainer's competency or deficiency in specialized areas and occasionally provide helpful data in making a well-researched wager. *Daily Racing Form* past performances cover several different categories known as "trainer form" underneath each horse's workouts, and list up to six of the most applicable categories.

These categories cover the trainer's starters since the beginning of the previous year. Generally, a winning benchmark of 15 percent or greater, and an ROI (return on investment) of $1.90 or higher in one category are considered above average and worthy of notice. At the present time, *Daily Racing Form* is tracking almost 40 types of trainer statistics. Each trainer stat lists (a) the number of starts for a trainer in each category; (b) the win percentage for the trainer in that category; and (c) the $2 ROI for the trainer in that category.

The complete list of comprehensive trainer stats includes the following, and the abbreviations indicated in parentheses are what appear under the past performances of each horse. The stats listed in bold indicate those that may be supportive in finding a favorable trainer pattern (angle) for a Derby entrant.

1. **First North American start**   **(1stNA)**
2. First race after claim   (1stClaim)
3. **First race with trainer**   **(1stW/Trn)**
4. **More than 180 days since last race**   **(+180Days)**
5. **61–180 days since last race**   **(61–180Days)**
6. **Second off a layoff of 45–180 Days**   **(2off45–180)**
7. **Second off a layoff of more than 180 days**   **(2offOver180)**
8. 1–7 days since last race   (1–7Days)
9. First-time starter   (1stStart)
10. Second starts with maidens (2ndStart)
11. Maiden special weight to maiden claimer   (MSWtoMCL)
12. First-time turf   (1stTurf)
13. First-time blinkers   (1stBlink)
14. First-time Lasix   (1stLasix)
15. 2-year-olds   (2YO)
16. Dirt to turf   (Dirt/Turf)
17. Turf to dirt   (Turf/Dirt)
18. Blinkers on   (BlinkOn)
19. Blinkers off   (BlinkOff)
20. Sprint to route   (Sprint/Route)
21. Route to sprint   (Route/Sprint)

22. Two sprints to a route — (2Sprints/Route)
23. 31–60 days since last race — (31–60 Days)
24. Won last start — (WonLastStart)
25. Dirt — (Dirt)
26. Turf — (Turf)
27. Sprints — (Sprints)
28. Routes — (Routes)
29. Maiden claiming — (MdnClm)
30. Maiden special weight — (MdnSpWt)
31. Claiming — (Claim)
32. Allowance — (Alw)
33. Stakes — (Stakes)
34. Graded stakes — (GrdStk)
35. Debut in maiden claimer — (DebutMCL)
36. Debut at a distance greater than or equal to one mile — (Debut>=1Mile)

Onesockmissing	Ch. c. 2 (Mar)		Life	2 M 0 0	$840 52	D.Fst	0 0 0 0	$0
Own: Cecil Robert Dean and Lafollette, Jos	Sire: Cat Thief (Storm Cat) $7,500					Wet(426)	0 0 0 0	$0
	Dam: Punching (Two Punch)		2007	2 M 0 0	$840 52	Synth	2 0 0 0	$840
	Br: Dean Cecil & Joseph Lafollette (Ky)		2006	0 M 0 0	$0 –	Turf(228)	0 0 0 0	$0
	Tr: Asmussen Steven M(219 60 45 23 .27) 2007:(2273 488 .21)		Fg	0 0 0 0	$0 –	Dst(384)	1 0 0 0	$840

25Aug07-3AP fst 6f ◇ :23 :46² :581 1:10¹ Md Sp Wt 28k 52 7 1 2½ 2½ 44½ 5¹⁰ Emigh C A L118 2.70 - - *Texas Fever*118⁵¾ Kabob118¹ Terryhowieandjimmy118²¼ Stalked used
14Jly07-6AP fst 5f ◇ :22³ :46³ :591 Md Sp Wt 28k 44 7 5 5³ 6³¾ 54 64 Graham J L118 14.50 - - *SebstinCounty*118¹ ActionSeeker118½ OutofthRuff118¹ Mid-pack, no rah
WORKS: Dec15 EvT 5f wf 1:03² B *13/33* Dec1 EvT 4f fst :52 B *32/48* Nov17 EvT 4f fst :53¹ B *57/65*
TRAINER: 61–180Days(230 .23 $1.98) MSWtoMCL (77 .27 $1.64) 2YO (648 .22 $1.64) Dirt (2877 .22 $1.63) Sprint (2095 .21 $1.55) MdnClm (280 .24 $1.42)

Training giant Steve Asmussen has broken several Thorough-bred-racing records over the years and nearly snapped his 0-for-7 Derby drought with the talented colt Curlin in 2007. Curlin was third in the Derby, victorious in the Preakness, and second in the final leg of the Triple Crown at Belmont Park. He later went on to an impressive and convincing win in the Breeders' Cup Classic in the fall over Monmouth Park's sea of slop. Asmussen frequently shows positive statistics in almost every training category. When he entered the 2-year-old colt Onesockmissing in a $50,000 maiden-claiming event at Fair Grounds in December 2007, it was easy to spot Asmussen's training accomplishments by looking at his trainer-form statistics. Asmussen was clicking at over 20 percent in all six relevant training-angle categories.

61–180 Days (230 **.23** $1.98)

MSWtoMCL (77 **.27** $1.64)

2YO (648 **.22** $1.64)

Dirt (2,877 **.22** $1.64)

Sprint (2,095 **.21** $1.55)

MdnClm (280 **.24** $1.42)

LEGENDARY DERBY JOCKEYS AND TRAINERS

The following chart lists the trainers that have accumulated the most Derby victories and the respective years they had starters.

TRAINERS—Most Kentucky Derby Victories

Name (Years)	Starters	1st	2nd	3rd	Off the Board
Ben A. Jones (1938–52)	11	6	2	1	2
D. Wayne Lukas (1981–2005)	42	4	1	5	32
H. J. "Dick" Thompson (1920–37)	24	4	2	1	17
"Sunny Jim" Fitzsimmons (1930–57)	11	3	1	0	7
Max Hirsch (1915–51)	14	3	0	2	9
Bob Baffert (1996–2006)	17	3	1	2	11
Lazaro Barrera (1976–90)	5	2	0	0	3
Henry Forest (1966–68)	2	2	0	0	0
LeRoy Jolley (1962–92)	13	2	2	1	8
H. A. "Jimmy" Jones (1956–58)	4	2	1	0	1
Lucien Laurin (1966–73)	5	2	0	1	2
Horatio Luro (1960–81)	4	2	0	1	1
John McGinty (N/A)	N/A	2	-	-	-
James Rowe Sr. (N/A-1925)	18	2	1	1	14
Woodford C. Stephens (1949–88)	14	2	3	3	6
Charles Whittingham (1958–96)	7	2	1	0	4
Nicholas P. Zito (1990–2005)	19	2	0	0	17

Hall of Fame jockeys Bill Hartack and Eddie Arcaro are the only riders with as many as *five* Kentucky Derby winners. The following chart lists the jockeys that have accumulated the most Derby victories and the respective years they had starters. Although he was one win shy of Arcaro and Hartack, fellow Hall of Famer Bill Shoemaker still holds the record for starters with an astounding 26, a mark that is likely to stand for many decades to come.

JOCKEYS—Most Kentucky Derby Victories

Name (Years)	Starters	1st	2nd	3rd	Unplaced
Eddie Arcaro (1935–61)	21	5	3	2	11
Bill Hartack (1956–74)	12	5	1	0	6
Bill Shoemaker (1952–88)	26	4	3	4	15
Angel Cordero Jr. (1968–91)	17	3	1	0	13
Gary Stevens (1985–2005)	18	3	2	1	12
Isaac Murphy (1877–93)	11	3	1	2	5
Earle Sande (1918–32)	8	3	2	0	3
Chris Antley (1988–99)	8	2	0	1	5
Jerry Bailey (1982–2005)	17	2	2	1	12
Eddie Delahoussaye (1975–2002)	13	2	2	2	7
Kent Desormeaux (1988–2007)	15	2	0	2	11
Albert Johnson (1922–28)	7	2	1	0	4
Charles Kurtsinger (1931–37)	4	2	0	1	1
Johnny Loftus (1912–19)	6	2	0	1	3
Linus McAtee (1920–29)	7	2	0	0	5
Chris McCarron (1976–2002)	18	2	3	0	13
Conn McCreary (1941–58)	10	2	0	2	6
Willie Simms (1896–98)	2	2	0	0	0
Ron Turcotte (1965–77)	5	2	0	1	2
Ismael Valenzuela (1958–74)	8	2	1	0	5
Jacinto Vasquez (1964–93)	9	2	0	0	7
Jimmy Winkfield (1900–03)	4	2	1	1	0

The success and failures of recent jockeys and trainers can be obtained by looking at the past 20 years. The following Derby jockeys and trainers have either had multiple wins in the last two decades, or they have yet to find the winner's circle despite several attempts.

Trainer D. Wayne Lukas (4 victories)

1999 Charismatic (Chris Antley)
1996 Grindstone (Jerry Bailey)
1995 Thunder Gulch (Gary Stevens)
1988 Winning Colors (Gary Stevens)

Trainer Bob Baffert (3 victories)

2002 War Emblem (Victor Espinoza)
1998 Real Quiet (Kent Desormeaux)
1997 Silver Charm (Gary Stevens)

Trainer Nick Zito (2 victories)

1994 Go for Gin (Chris MCarron)
1991 Strike the Gold (Chris Antley)

Trainer Carl Nafzger (2 victories)

2007 Street Sense (Calvin Borel)
1990 Unbridled (Craig Perret)

The Derby Goose-Egg Club

*(*The following trainers and jockeys are still active)*
Trainer Todd Pletcher (0 for 19)
Trainer John Kimmel (0 for 12)
Trainer Robert Frankel (0 for 8)
Trainer Steve Asmussen (0 for 7)
Trainer Ron McAnally (0 for 7)
Trainer Saeed bin Suroor (0 for 5)
Trainer Richard Mandella (0 for 5)
Trainer Shug McGaughey (0 for 4)

Jockey Alex Solis (0 for 14)
Jockey Corey Nakatani (0 for 13)
Jockey Robby Albarado (0 for 9)
Jockey David Flores (0 for 9)
Jockey John Velazquez Jr. (0 for 8)
Jockey Mark Guidry (0 for 5)
Jockey Garrett Gomez (0 for 4)
Jockey Ramon Dominguez (0 for 4)

Four-time Eclipse Award winner Todd Pletcher broke his own North American earnings record in 2007 with a season total of roughly $27 million. A perennial leader in New York, Pletcher won five consecutive Saratoga training titles from 2002 through 2006. He has also held training titles at Belmont Park, Aqueduct, Gulfstream Park, and Keeneland. In 2007, he equaled the record for sending out the most starters in a single Derby when he saddled five entrants, but not one of them hit the board. Despite his astonishing success in almost every other Thoroughbred-racing category, Pletcher's record in the Kentucky Derby stands at 0 for 19.

IMPORTANCE OF GRADE 1 TRAINING SUCCESS

IF YOU ARE enthusiastic about wagering on a Derby starter that is trained by a Derby newbie, it is highly recommended that you at least look for a trainer who has been reasonably successful in other high-profile graded stakes across the country and has accumulated a high overall win percentage. The following charts list the top 25 jockeys and trainers based on performance in Grade 1 races over the past three years, from the beginning of 2005 to the end of 2007.

The trainers and jockeys listed below are arranged by number of Grade 1 victories. Grade 1's are the highest class of race in this country. If your trainer or jockey has made this list, it's more than likely that he is qualified to have a horse in the Derby.

JOCKEYS—American Grade 1 Stakes Races

Name	Starters	1st	2nd	3rd	ROI
Garrett Gomez	156	32	25	17	2.46
John R. Velazquez Jr.	154	29	29	19	1.22
Edgar S. Prado	137	23	17	19	1.62
Corey S. Nakatani	111	19	12	13	1.81
Cornelio H. Velasquez	95	11	14	13	1.87
Alex Solis	86	11	15	9	0.85
Robby Albarado	55	8	9	5	2.73
Kent J. Desormeaux	77	7	10	9	2.70
Eibar Coa	63	7	6	2	0.87
Mike E. Smith	58	6	3	10	3.40

BIG-DAY JOCKEYS AND TRAINERS

Name	Starters	1st	2nd	3rd	ROI
David R. Flores	45	6	12	8	1.02
Calvin H. Borel	25	6	5	4	11.10
Patrick A. Valenzuela	64	5	10	10	0.91
John K. Court	41	5	3	6	2.96
*Jose A. Santos (retired)	34	4	5	2	2.90
Michael J. Luzzi	33	4	3	6	1.68
Rene R. Douglas	35	4	2	3	1.71
Mathew O. McCarron	17	4	2	4	0.66
Richard Migliore	45	3	6	6	1.71
Lanfranco Dettori	15	2	0	2	1.89
Mario G. Pino	13	2	4	4	1.34
Mark Guidry	40	2	6	2	3.96
Martin A. Pedroza	27	2	2	3	0.94
John P. Murtagh	9	1	2	1	0.53
Russell A. Baze	7	1	1	0	0.37

TRAINERS—American Grade 1 Stakes Races

Name	Starters	1st	2nd	3rd	ROI
Todd A. Pletcher	230	44	40	30	1.65
Robert J. Frankel	141	22	21	16	1.32
Bob Baffert	59	15	5	9	1.94
Doug F. O'Neill	94	14	5	9	1.63
Kiaran P. McLaughlin	53	14	14	7	3.17
Richard E. Dutrow, Jr.	56	11	8	6	2.21
Richard E. Mandella	29	8	3	5	3.63
William I. Mott	57	7	1	6	1.18
John A. Shirreffs	34	7	2	5	5.95
Neil D. Drysdale	43	6	7	5	1.49
Nicholas P. Zito	90	6	15	14	0.58
Claude R. McGaughey III	31	6	9	2	3.78
Sanna N. Hendriks	17	6	1	2	0.00
Patrick L. Biancone	75	4	10	10	0.47
Steven M. Asmussen	35	4	5	5	1.06
Christophe Clement	26	4	3	4	2.78
David E. Hofmans	23	4	4	3	1.52
Paul D. Fout	22	4	2	5	0.51
Barclay Tagg	19	4	2	2	1.36

Name	Starters	1st	2nd	3rd	ROI
Carl A. Nafzger	17	4	6	1	3.41
Jeff Mullins	16	4	1	1	5.29
Thomas Albertrani	18	3	4	2	1.82
Dan L. Hendricks	15	3	1	0	1.69
Ronald L. McAnally	27	3	4	3	1.12
Julio C. Canani	32	3	1	3	1.09

8

DERBY BETTING AND THE BASIC WAGERING PROCESS

IT'S ASTONISHING THAT many seasoned bettors still have no clue how parimutuel betting actually works. The old cliché that the track is "getting over" or getting rich at the expense of the racing public is some type of old-school thinking that appears to be set in granite. A substantial segment of the wagering community still incorrectly assumes that the track makes more money when a 2–5 shot finishes 11th of 12 and some 74–1 shot lights up the tote board.

Contrary to what many people believe, wagering on a parimutuel event such as horse racing or greyhound racing is not like wagering at a casino. "Parimutuel" is a term that comes from the French phrase "among ourselves." It means that you and other bettors wager among one another in common pools, not against the track.

In fact, racetrack proprietors have no interest in the result of the race, and the track deducts a statutory commission from each dollar wagered, similar to a stockbroker's commission, regardless of the outcome. Every dollar bet at the racetrack, minus the small percentage of "takeout" that gets split between the track and state government, is returned to the members of the betting public who hold winning tickets after each race.

The takeout, or retention rate, varies from state to state, track to track, and by the type of wager. It can be as low as 15 percent for a win bet, or as high as 35 percent for an exotic wager. The amount the track retains is its revenue, which is used to pay race purses, taxes, salaries, and other operating expenses. As mentioned above, the remaining percentage goes back to the public in what is known as common pools. Each type of wager has a specific common pool and there are multiple pools on every race. For instance, trifecta wagers go into a trifecta pool, and all exacta wagers go into an exacta pool.

The odds shown on the tote board are a reflection of the handicapping opinion of bettors that have invested in a particular race. The total amount that gets paid after a race is declared official is the remainder of the amount bet in the pool after the takeout. Unlike casino games, horse-racing odds are not predetermined and merely reflect the opinion of the wagering public. The more money wagered on a horse, the lower the payoff. The less money wagered on a horse, the higher the payoff. The goal for you as a bettor is to find discrepancies between a horse's odds and his actual chances of winning. That's easier said than done.

Anyone can pick a race favorite, and every race has one. In the long run, however, betting on favorites and short-priced horses is a losing proposition, and the reward is far less than the risk. It's important to think of the betting process as one of risk versus reward. If you wager on "favorites" who have a solid shot of winning based on their past performances, you're likely to cash more tickets. However, the return on investment (ROI) will be lower, because many of your fellow handicappers will have backed the same logical contenders. Conversely, when you wager on longshots—horses whose past performances indicate they have only a remote chance of winning—you'll cash fewer tickets, but the return on investment will be much greater, because only a small fraction of the public will share equally in the total amount of money bet on the race.

It is important to remember that the odds for each runner are not necessarily the same thing as an entrant's actual chances of winning the race. The odds simply stand for the betting public's *opinion* of who will win. Over many years, documented parimutuel analysis shows that favorites (entrants with the most money bet on them) win at an amazingly consistent rate of 33 percent. That figure is one of the few universal betting standards.

Backing post-time favorites in the Kentucky Derby has not exactly been a lucrative betting strategy, but it has succeeded at a slightly higher rate than betting the chalk in other day-to-day races. Out of 133 runnings, 51 post-time favorites (38 percent) have won the Kentucky Derby, and the 2007 winner, Street Sense ($11.80; 4.90–1) was a slight favorite over third-place finisher Curlin (5–1). Street Sense was the third winning favorite in the last eight years, but before that, there had been a drought in that category that stretched back to Spectacular Bid in 1979. The results from the last 20 Derbies have proven that value still exists in the win pool, with the average winner hovering somewhere around 12–1.

2007	Street Sense	*$11.80
2006	Barbaro	$14.20
2005	Giacomo	$102.60
2004	Smarty Jones	*$10.20
2003	Funny Cide	$27.60
2002	War Emblem	$43.00
2001	Monarchos	$23.00
2000	Fusaichi Pegasus	*$6.60
1999	Charismatic	$64.60
1998	Real Quiet	$18.80
1997	Silver Charm	$10.00
1996	Grindstone	$13.80
1995	Thunder Gulch	$51.00
1994	Go for Gin	$20.20
1993	Sea Hero	$27.80
1992	Lil E. Tee	$35.60
1991	Strike the Gold	$11.60
1990	Unbridled	$23.60
1989	Sunday Silence	$8.20
1988	Winning Colors	$8.80

Average Payoff: **$26.60**

Indicates race favorite

There have been some dazzling win payoffs in the history of the Derby, which certainly provides evidence that it is still one of the greatest betting opportunities of the year. The 2005 Derby winner,

Giacomo, was the most recent of a select group of Derby winners that paid triple digits. Some of the largest payoffs of all time include:

Year	Horse	Payoff
1913	Donerail	$184.90
2005	Giacomo	$102.60
1940	Gallahadion	$72.40
1999	Charismatic	$64.60
1967	Proud Clarion	$62.20
1918	Exterminator	$61.20
1953	Dark Star	$51.80
1995	Thunder Gulch	$51.00
1908	Stone Street	$49.40
1982	Gato del Sol	$44.40

With a few exceptions, it makes little handicapping and financial sense to back a Derby favorite. There are several reasons why you should try and beat the public's choice in the Run for the Roses, but the simplest explanation for attempting to do so is that the best horse doesn't always win America's most grueling race.

With a field size averaging somewhere between 16 and 18 horses, the likelihood for a rough or troublesome trip increases tenfold. In addition, these developing 3-year-olds are attempting to navigate a distance they have no previous experience with. One of the principles of everyday "Handicapping 101" is that it usually does not make sense to take short odds on a horse that is attempting to do something he is trying for the first time. Some common examples include a horse stretching out to a route, changing racing surfaces (turf to dirt; dirt to turf; dirt to a synthetic surface; synthetic to dirt), carrying excessive weight, or being asked to compete on very short rest.

STRAIGHT BETS: BETTING TO WIN, PLACE, AND SHOW

BETTING TO WIN, place, and show should be fairly easy to comprehend, and experienced handicappers might want to skip to the next chapter, which addresses the topic of multi-race bets and putting yourself in position to make a life-changing Derby score on a wide variety of superexotics. But for now, here are the basics.

In order for you to cash a win bet, your horse needs to win the race. This is the preferred betting strategy for millions of casual bettors. Win payoffs, like most bets, correlate to field size and the competitiveness of a specific race. Larger fields—such as those you typically see in the Kentucky Derby—include more potential results, and therefore, elevated payoffs.

There's nothing wrong with playing a horse to win in the Kentucky Derby. The large and competitive field ensures overlay win odds and optimum betting opportunities. The sharpest bettors on normal race days want a certain minimum payoff on their selected horse, and many will pass a race if they can't get their price. A good starting point and recommendation for the Derby is that you not back your selection to win unless you are receiving at least 9–2 or 5–1 in the win pool.

Finding value and "overlays" is the name of the game in the win pool. For example, if a horse is 8–1 on the tote board and the bettor thinks the horse should be 4–1, that person has found an overlay, or a horse that will pay more than it should, based on sound handicapping. This example represents decent value. Conversely, when a horse is 8–5 on the board and the bettor believes the horse should be 5–1, he has spotted an "underlay," or a horse that will pay less than it should to win—poor value and generally a bad bet.

Over the long haul, it is essential to pursue horses that represent good value in order to make up for the bets you do not win. Logically, the path to profitable win betting is to know your own percentage of picking winners and then have the patience to wait for the right horses at the right prices. Cashing tickets requires identifying feeble spots in the betting pools and swooping in to take your piece of the pie when the price is right. The general public is right approximately 33 percent of the time, but that also means they are wrong more than 66 percent of the time.

Betting to place allows you to cash a ticket if your choice runs first *or* second. A show bet means you win if your selection runs first, second, *or* third. Although the actual odds to place and show are not shown on the tote board or television monitors, you can use the win odds as a *very rough* estimate of what these bets on the lesser positions will pay. In general, place payoffs average one-third of the win price. Show payoffs return about one-sixth of the win odds.

As we already mentioned, betting to show means that your horse can finish first, second, or third. Payoffs vary depending on the amount wagered to show on the horses that finish first, second, and third. If a solid favorite manages to hit the board, the show payoffs will be significantly depleted because the favorite usually has the most money bet on him to show.

As *Daily Racing Form* West Coast handicapper Brad Free wrote in his book *Handicapping 101: A Horse-Racing Primer* (DRF Press; 2007), "Betting to place is tedious, payoffs are low, and it's difficult to formulate a winning strategy." The same can be said for show betting. They are both losing propositions and not recommended on Derby Day, or any other racing day, for that matter. If you find yourself contemplating a place or show wager against a solid favorite, you'd be much better off playing to win or betting an exacta or trifecta— or even skipping the race altogether if you think that your longshot selection's chance of beating the public's choice is slim. Plenty of other betting opportunities are always right around the corner.

Another common and basic betting strategy is win-place wagering. When you make a win-place bet, your horse must finish first or second in order for you to cash your ticket. If your horse wins you collect both the win payoff and the place payoff. If your horse finishes second you collect only the place payoff. Obviously it is better if your horse wins, but the additional place option in this type of bet offers you a chance to recoup some of your investment if your horse fails to win but still finishes second.

Finally, the most popular straight bet is betting across the board. When you bet a horse across the board, he must finish first, second, or third in order for you to cash your ticket. If your horse wins, you collect all three payoffs—win, place, and show. If your horse finishes second, you collect the place and show payoffs only. If your horse finishes third, you collect only the show payoff. As with win-place wagering, this offers you a chance to get something back if your horse fails to win but still finishes second or third.

TRANSLATING WIN ODDS INTO DOLLAR VALUES

THE ODDS AS listed on the tote board or on television monitors show how much an entrant will pay to win based on every dollar wagered. For example, a minimum $2 bet on a runner who wins at 5–1 odds will pay $12, because you win $5 for each dollar bet (5 x 2 = 10), *plus* when you win you always get back the original cost of your bet ($10 winnings + the original $2 bet = $12).

Some win odds are listed as fractions and should be read as such: 7–2 odds equals $7 won for every $2 invested, which is the same as saying the odds were $3^1/2$–1; 9–5 odds equals $9 won for every $5 invested, which is the same as saying the odds were $1^4/5$–1. The chart below is a quick reference for common odds and their returns until you become familiar with calculating payoffs. If you have a difficult time understanding what your winning selection is going to pay, keep the chart close by for easy reference. You'd be amazed how many bettors don't know the difference between an 8–5 and a 2–1 shot.

Win Payoffs Based on $2 Wagers

Odds	Payoff	Odds	Payoff
1–9	$2.20	1–5	$2.40
2–5	$2.80	1–2	$3.00
3–5	$3.20	4–5	$3.60
1–1 (or "even")	$4.00	6–5	$4.40
7–5	$4.80	3–2	$5.00
8–5	$5.20	9–5	$5.60
2–1	$6.00	5–2	$7.00
3–1	$8.00	7–2	$9.00
4–1	$10.00	9–2	$11.00
5–1	$12.00	6–1	$14.00
7–1	$16.00	8–1	$18.00
9–1	$20.00	10–1	$22.00
15–1	$32.00	20–1	$42.00
30–1	$62.00	40–1	$82.00
50–1	$102.00	100–1	$202.00

9

INTRA-RACE AND
MULTI-RACE BETTING

WITH NEARLY $120 million bet on the Kentucky Derby each year, the wagering opportunities are plentiful. Many seasoned bettors welcome Derby Day like a 5-year-old having full domain over Goofy's Candy Co. The Derby wagering menu offers enough candy for everyone who wants to participate, and for many gamblers it's a chance to make a life-changing score. Today's horseplayer has a tremendous opportunity that was not available to his betting counterpart of two or three decades ago—a vast array of options beyond the traditional win, place, and show discussed in Chapter 8.

The betting menu has certainly changed over the last several decades. The most notable difference involves exotic bets. If you are a novice handicapper, you might not be aware of what exotic bets are, or how to place them. Whether you intend to be a track regular or are planning a one-day visit to Churchill Downs, the following tips on intra-race and multi-race wagers should be very useful.

The goal for all bettors at all wagering levels should be to cash in on the inflated big-race-day pools, which are frequently flooded with recreational and uniformed dollars. Once you understand which wagers are the most "bettor friendly," you'll be on your way to navigating the full Derby betting menu for a memorable and profitable afternoon.

There are now two basic types of horse-racing bets—straight bets and exotic bets. Straight bets include win, place, and show and were discussed in the previous chapter. Exotic bets can be divided into two categories—intra-race bets and multi-race bets. The intra-race bets, which allow multi-horse wagering on individual races, include exactas, quinellas, trifectas, and superfectas.

The multi-race bets, which require a bettor to select the winners of consecutive races, include the daily double, pick three, pick four, pick five, and pick six.

The most traditional and basic multi-race bet is the daily double, which involves picking the winners for two consecutive races. All tracks have a daily double on their exotic wagering menu. There is usually an early daily double on the first and second races, and a late daily double on the last two races. Several racetracks, particularly in Southern California, "roll" the daily double throughout the card. This simply means that the daily-double bet is available on all races throughout the day. (For instance, race 1 and race 2; race 2 and race 3; etc.)

GETTING EXOTIC

BETTING ON HORSE RACING was simple 30 to 40 years ago, when the only available wagers were straight bets (win, place, and show). It was even easier hundreds of years ago when winning was all that mattered. "You've got a horse, I've got a horse—I bet my horse can beat your horse."

Today, the availability of exotic wagering allows you to turn an otherwise unplayable race into a prime betting opportunity by combining horses on a single ticket in the same race, or over multiple races in a manner that will produce an overlay payoff. A bettor no longer has to pass a race when his three-star best bet of the day is 7–5. The beauty of exotic wagering is that big profits are obtainable for sharp bettors and handicappers who can properly structure multi-horse and multi-race bets.

Today, multiple and exotic bets account for more than 65 percent of the handle because they offer the prospect of turning a small or medium-size investment into a large and sometimes life-changing payout. Furthermore, these wagers allow the bettor to spread the effect of racetrack takeout over several races, so you are actually facing a smaller takeout percentage per race than you would if the race were played separately.

As racing became more modernized in the early 20th century, place and show betting were added to the wagering menu, allowing those with smaller bankrolls to make safer yet lower-paying bets on horses to finish second or third. Finally, the daily double emerged, an exotic wager requiring you to pick the winners of two consecutive races. Those limited choices remained the same for decades until the exacta and quinella were developed. The exacta required bettors to pick the first two finishers in a race in exact order, and the quinella required them to pick the first two finishers in a race in either order. These bets were the first of the new exotic wagers to be added to many track wagering menus in an effort to spice up potential payoffs and compete with other forms of gambling. These two wagers were commonplace at many tracks by the late 1970s and early 1980s.

The 1980s also ushered in the pick six, a multi-race bet that involved picking the winners of six consecutive races on one ticket. The pick six was followed by the pick three and the "win four," or pick four. The pick three and pick four gave bettors with smaller bankrolls a chance at the large potential payoffs previously available only to pick-six players. Although the pick six is available at many racing circuits throughout the country, the bigger and more attractive pools are commonplace in New York and Southern California.

Trifectas, which required bettors to pick the first three finishers in a race in exact order, also became popular and are now commonplace at every track on almost every race. The superfecta was developed next, offering the lure of huge payouts for picking the first four finishers in a race in exact order.

Listed below are some common exotic wagers available at Churchill Downs on Kentucky Oaks Day and Derby Day, along with some helpful tips and angles for playing each exotic bet. This large and attractive betting menu offers endless possibilities to not only make your betting experience more exciting, but hopefully that much more profitable.

QUINELLA, EXACTA, TRIFECTA, AND SUPERFECTA

INTRA-RACE BETS require you to pick multiple horses in the same race to finish in the first two to four positions. Sound impossible? With fundamental handicapping and some simple betting techniques, it's not as intimidating as you might think. Although these types of exotic bets are slightly more difficult to plan and execute than straight bets, they also offer greater opportunities to win large amounts of money.

While straight bets have been around for hundreds of years, resulting in an efficient market, intra-race and multi-race exotic-betting options have been around for far less time. Many bettors have not yet learned how to properly structure exotic-wagering tickets, resulting in inefficiencies in the betting pools that can be exploited by smart handicappers and bettors. These lucrative betting pools are available tenfold on Derby Day and are simply loaded with overlay opportunities. It pays to understand intra-race and multi-race exotic wagering and leave the win, place, and show betting to the less informed patrons in the Derby crowd, who are busy sipping mint juleps, socializing with friends and relatives, and betting on their favorite colors and family-pet names.

Exacta: Exacta betting requires you to pick the first- and second-place finishers in a race in exact order. A "box" allows you to reverse this order of finish, but also doubles the cost of the bet. A "wheel" means you play a single entrant in either the first or second spot with all the others in the race. A "partial wheel," or "part-wheel," allows you to select two or more other horses to finish first or second with your single. For example, if you play a $2 exacta, 11–15, the 11 horse must win and the 15 horse must finish second in order for you to cash a ticket. A popular option is to play a multiple-horse exacta box. For example, a $2 exacta box of horses 11 and 15 (at a cost of $4) would include two combinations. With this type of wager you would win if the order of finish was either 11–15 or 15–11. Exacta wagering offers casual and professional players alike the chance of making a good score with a minimal outlay of cash. In 2005, the $2 exacta of winner Giacomo and runner-up Closing Argument returned a whopping $9,814.80, a Derby-record payoff.

$2 Exacta Box: A box includes every combination of the runners selected. You collect when any two runners in the box finish first and second, in either order in the race. An exacta box based on a $2 wager costs $12 for a three-runner combination.

Number of Runners	Number of Bets	Total Cost
3	6	$12
4	12	$24
5	20	$40
6	30	$60
7	42	$84
8	56	$112

Trifecta: Trifecta betting requires you to pick the first-, second-, and third-place finishers in a race in exact order. For example, if you play a $2 straight trifecta of horses 1, 2, and 3, the 1 horse must win, the 2 horse must finish second, and the 3 horse must finish third. A common option is to play a multiple-horse trifecta box. For example, a $1 trifecta box of horses 1, 2, and 3 (at a cost of $6) would include six possible $1 combinations and would pay off if those horses finished in the first three positions in any order. Trifecta wagering, while obviously more risky, offers all bettors the chance of making a big score. There are numerous different methods of betting trifectas, some more efficient than others. Although the trifecta box is the easiest to comprehend and the most common, it is *not* the best betting option available. By boxing, you are giving each horse an equal chance of winning, and that's an amateurish way to think and bet. In 2005, the $2 trifecta of Giacomo, Closing Argument, and Afleet Alex returned an incredible $133,134.80, which was a Derby-record trifecta payoff and an indication of how rewarding this intra-race exotic bet can be on Derby Day.

$1 Trifecta Box: Boxing allows the bettor to select three or more runners in all possible combinations. A three-horse trifecta box based on a $1 wager costs $6. It returns half of the $2 trifecta payout. If the selections you boxed finished first, second, and third in any order, you win.

Number of Runners	Number of Bets	Total Cost
3	6	$6
4	24	$24
5	60	$60
6	120	$120
7	210	$210
8	336	$336

$1 Trifecta Wheel: The trifecta "wheel" is a much better option than boxing. With the wheel, you select the horse that you feel has the best chance of finishing first, second, or third, and tell the mutuel clerk to wheel that runner in the position you have chosen with all the other entrants. If your horse finishes in the position you selected, you collect one-half of the $2 trifecta price. The finish of all the other entrants does not matter. The trifecta wheel is an option when you find a horse that you think has an excellent chance of hitting the board at overlaid odds, but you don't necessarily think he is good enough to win the race. The wheel allows you to play this 30–1 or 40–1 shot in the second or third position and surround him with all other contenders for a handsome payout. Although wheeling is generally less expensive than boxing, the cost can still mount quickly: For example, wheeling one horse with "all/all" in an eight-horse field would cost $42 (1 x 7 x 6).

$1 Trifecta Key: The trifecta "key" is a trimmer version of the wheel. If you bet a trifecta key, you must state exactly where you think your key horse will finish: first, second, or third. He must finish in the position you select in order for you to collect. Unlike the wheel, which allows you to use *all* the remaining entrants, the trifecta key is a more assertive betting approach in that you are surrounding your selection with contenders you think have a legitimate chance to fill out the trifecta. The cost of a $1 trifecta key is as follows:

Number of Runners	Number of Bets	Total Cost
Key 1 with 2 others	2	$2
Key 1 with 3 others	6	$6
Key 1 with 4 others	12	$12

Number of Runners	Number of Bets	Total Cost
Key 1 with 5 others	20	$20
Key 1 with 6 others	30	$30
Key 1 with 7 others	42	$42

Superfecta: Superfectas require you to pick the first-, second-, third-, and fourth-place finishers in a race in exact order. For example, if you play a $1 straight superfecta, 2–3–4–5, the 2 horse must win, the 3 horse must finish second, the 4 horse must finish third, and the 5 horse must finish fourth. A high-risk/high-return proposition, superfecta betting can be quite expensive, but it does offer the potential for life-changing payouts. Playing superfecta boxes that include multiple horses can be both pricey and unproductive, but as shown with the trifecta, other methods such as wheels and part-wheels can offer you a good chance of winning a substantial sum for a more reasonable outlay. In addition, many racetracks have implemented the ever-growing and popular 10-cent superfecta, which allows the bettor a tremendous amount of wagering coverage at just a fraction of the usual cost. The 2005 Kentucky Derby was a memorable exotics bonanza. The $2 superfecta of Giacomo, Closing Argument, Afleet Alex, and Don't Get Mad returned an incredible $864,253.50.

$1 Superfecta Box: You must select four (or more) horses you think have the best chance of finishing first, second, third, and fourth. Like the $1 trifecta box, the $1 superfecta box returns one-half of the $2 payoff. A minimum four-horse box (24 total bets) costs $24, and the cost of the bet increases significantly with each additional runner.

Number of Runners	Number of Bets	Total Cost
4	24	$24
5	120	$120
6	360	$360
7	840	$840
8	1,680	$1,680

$1 Superfecta Key: In playing the superfecta key you must state which position you think your horse will occupy: first, second, third, or fourth. He must obviously finish in the position you select in order for you to cash.

Number of Runners	Number of Bets	Total Cost
Key 1 with 3 others	6	$6
Key 1 with 4 others	24	$24
Key 1 with 5 others	60	$60
Key 1 with 6 others	120	$120
Key 1 with 7 others	210	$210

MULTI-RACE BETTING OPTIONS:
DAILY DOUBLE, PICK THREE, PICK FOUR, AND PICK SIX

THE MOST COMMON multi-race bets—the daily double, pick three, pick four, and pick six—require you to pick the winners of consecutive races. There are a few significant advantages to playing multi-race wagers. As mentioned earlier, the first of these is the fact that each multi-race wager has its own betting pool. The government and racetrack takeout is applied to a multi-race bet only once, despite that fact that the bet occurs over two or more races. In contrast, a separate win bet on each race would be subject to the government and track takeout each time. So while multiple-race wagers inherently have more risk, they also offer better odds, partly due to a takeout that occurs only once rather than on each race.

The second advantage to multi-race wagers is the fact that the public tends to overbet certain combinations. As with intra-race wagering, many amateur and inexperienced bettors do not know how to structure multi-race tickets properly. This results in excellent value-based opportunities for better-informed handicappers and bettors.

Daily Double: The daily double was the first exotic-wagering option at racetracks in North America. This bet requires you to select the winner of two consecutive races. For example, if you play a $2 daily double, 11–6, the 11 horse must win the first race in the sequence and the 6 horse must win the second. Many bettors opt for a $2 daily-double wheel, which allows them to use one horse (or sometimes more) in one leg of the wager while using all horses in the other leg. For example, a $2 daily-double wheel of the 11 in the first race with the 1, 2, 3, 4, 5, 6, 7, and 8 in the second race would include eight possible combinations at a cost of $16. A part-wheel would narrow your selections to fewer horses.

Daily doubles are traditionally offered on the first two races of the card, but many racetracks now offer both an early and a late double, and some tracks even offer rolling daily doubles throughout the card—e.g. races 1 and 2, races 2 and 3, races 3 and 4, and so on. Because the daily double is the oldest of the multi-race wagers, it's very popular among longtime racegoers. Occasionally doubles are offered on important stakes races contested on separate days. The most prominent and popular example is the traditional "Oaks-Derby Double" offered by Churchill Downs, where bettors pick the winners of the Kentucky Oaks and the Kentucky Derby.

Pick Three: The pick three offers an excellent opportunity for a high-quality score with a minimal outlay of cash. The pick three and pick four are two of my favorite betting options on Derby Day and should be your desired wagers as well, provided that you have a good, strong opinion on a series of races on the Oaks or Derby card. As its name implies, the pick three requires you to select the winners of three consecutive races. For example, a $2 straight pick three of 5, 1, and 9 would require a victory by horse 5 in the first race (or leg) of the pick three, horse 1 in the second leg, and horse 9 in the third leg.

A popular but ill-advised pick-three strategy is the $1 pick-three wheel. For example, if you were to play a $1 pick-three wheel linking horses 8, 9, and 10 in the first leg to horses 2 and 3 in the second leg and horse 4 in the third leg (8, 9, 10 with 2, 3 with 4) at a cost of $6 (3 horses x 2 horses x 1 horse = 6 possible combinations), horse 8, 9, or 10 must win the first race of the sequence, horse 2 or 3 must win the second race, and horse 4 (the single) must win the third race in order for you to cash. You may use as many finishers in each leg of the sequence as you like, but each additional entrant increases the cost of the ticket exponentially.

A more effective betting approach is to play one "main" ticket with your two or three top contenders, along with some backup tickets using a third or fourth horse in each leg with your top three or four choices in the other two legs. This enhanced strategy, outlined below, gives the player an opportunity to include an obscure longshot in the sequence and can cause your pick-three payoff to skyrocket. This is a much more clever way to use your bankroll, since the horses selected as your main contenders are likely to be the same as those of the guy sitting beside you, and these types of logical candidates will be heavily used in most of the ticket combinations purchased.

	First Leg	Second Leg	Third Leg
Main Contenders:	A, B	A, B	A, B
Backup Contenders:	C, D	C, D	C, D

In the following pick-three betting example, four separate tickets are purchased for a total of $32, using $1 increments. We will use two main contenders and two backup contenders in each race. The main and backup-ticket approach allows for more coverage and less betting capital. The same design and approach can be used for both the pick four and the pick six.

Main Ticket: AB, AB, AB (2 x 2 x 2) = $8
Backup Ticket: CD, AB, AB (2 x 2 x 2) = $8
Backup Ticket: AB, CD, AB (2 x 2 x 2) = $8
Backup Ticket: AB, AB, CD (2 x 2 x 2) = $8

Many tracks, including Churchill Downs, now offer rolling pick threes on consecutive races throughout the race card—for example, races 3, 4, and 5; races 4, 5, and 6; races 5, 6, and 7, etc. There are a variety of ways to play this bet that can give you an advantage over your fellow horseplayers. One such method is to take advantage of bad betting favorites in the sequence, and hopefully get them out of the win slot in one or two races. If you can uncover an opportunity where a favorite appears susceptible, that is an excellent place to jump in and build a pick-three ticket around the potential public underlay.

Pick Four: The pick four offers both casual and professional players a chance at a four-figure score with a moderate outlay of money, and the bet has quickly become one of the most popular wagers in American racing. It is especially attractive on Derby Day and some other big-race days, when there is often a $1 million or $2 million guaranteed pool up for grabs and usually at least two pick fours on the betting menu.

As the name indicates, the pick four requires you to select the winner of four consecutive races. For example, a $2 straight pick four of 7, 8, 9, and 13 would require a win by horse 7 in the first leg, horse 8 in the second leg, horse 9 in the third, and horse 13 in the final leg. As with the pick three, wheeling is a popular plan of attack when novices play the pick four. For example, if you play a $1 pick-four part-wheel combining horses 3 and 4 in the first leg with horses 5 and 6 in the second leg, horses 7 and 8 in the third leg, and horses 9 and 10 in the fourth leg (3, 4 with 5, 6 with 7, 8 with 9, 10) at a cost of $16 ($1 x 2 horses x 2 horses x 2 horses x 2 horses = 16 possible combinations), horse 3 or 4 must win the first leg of the pick four, horse 5 or 6 must win the second leg, horse 7 or 8 must win the third leg, and horse 9 or 10 must win the fourth and final leg in order for you to collect. Once again, you may use as many runners in each leg of the sequence as you like, but each additional entrant increases the cost of the ticket exponentially.

It's strongly recommended that you save a large portion of your Derby bankroll for this multi-race bet. It's well worth the investment with the opportunity for gargantuan payoffs. The best strategy is to structure the bet like the pick three, with main and backup contenders. This extensive coverage will provide you with the most bang for your buck. Some racetracks offer a 50-cent minimum pick four, which allows the player to use even more combinations. At the $1 minimum it is highly recommended that you "spread" by using several horses in some or all of the races in the hope of catching one or two longshots that will ultimately shape the size of your payoff. Here's a simple ticket example.

	First Leg	Second Leg	Third Leg	Fourth Leg
Main Contenders:	A, B, C	A, B	A, B	A, B, C, D
Backup Contenders:	D	C, D	C, D, E	F, G, H

In the following pick-four betting example, five separate tickets are purchased for a total of $220, using $1 increments.

Using all these horses in a $1 wheel would cost more than double at $560 (4 x 4 x 5 x 7), thus proving the advantage of main and backup tickets.

Main Ticket: ABC, AB, AB, ABCD (3 x 2 x 2 x 4) = $48
Backup Ticket: D, AB, AB, ABCD (1 x 2 x 2 x 4) = $16
Backup Ticket: ABC, CD, AB, ABCD (3 x 2 x 2 x 4) = $48
Backup Ticket: ABC, AB, CDE, ABCD (3 x 2 x 3 x 4) = $72
Backup Ticket: ABC, AB, AB, FGH (3 x 2 x 2 x 3) = $36

Pick Six: The pick six offers all types of bettors a chance to make a life-changing score. It is the most expensive of the exotic multi-race bets, but it is not uncommon to see five- or six-figure payoffs on a daily basis. Generally appealing to those with a larger bankroll, the pick six requires you to pick the winners of six consecutive races—an extremely challenging task. While playing the pick six as a straight $2 ticket using one horse per race offers a chance at the big money, the odds of winning using this method are astronomical—about like playing your state's Lotto. For example, if each race in a pick six had an eight-horse field, the odds of a straight $2 ticket coming in might be calculated as 8 x 8 x 8 x 8 x 8 x 8 = 262,144 combinations, or 262,144-to-1. Of course, since every horse in the race does not have an equal chance of winning, the odds can be reduced accordingly, based on your selections and their relative chances of success. And since no bettor can afford to cover all 262,144 combinations, or even the thousands of semilogical combinations, a single horse, or key, must often be used in one or more races of the pick six in order to make the ticket affordable for the average Joe.

As an example, let's say you find two races in the pick six in which you really like one horse, and a few other races where you can narrow down the contenders. Your $2 pick-six partwheel ticket might look like this: 2 with 4, 9, 11 with 3, 6 with 1 with 2, 3, 4 with 5, 6. The cost would be $72 (1 x 3 x 2 x 1 x 3 x 2 = 36 combinations x $2), which is certainly affordable. A popular method of playing the pick six is for several bettors to combine their financial resources—form a "syndicate"—in an effort to cover more combinations. Multiple $2 pick-six tickets costing in the range of $5,000 to $10,000 are not uncommon when a heavily bankrolled syndicate is trying to bring down a six-figure payout. The pick six is not recommended for the faint of heart or for the average player with a tight bankroll, thus making most Derby bettors and onlookers noneligible. However, the pick three and four are much more realistic and lucrative multi-race betting opportunities and can offer some mammoth payoffs for much less of an investment.

As you can see, exotic wagers can become very costly and complicated rather quickly, but they certainly create a lot of excitement compared to traditional win, place, and show wagering.

10

IN-THE-BLACK FRIDAY: THE OAKS

WHEN A DALLAS Stewart-trained 3-year-old filly named Lemons Forever came from last in a field of 14 to rally eight-wide and win the 132nd running of the Kentucky Oaks at 47–1, I had almost forgotten that the 2006 Kentucky Derby was still 24 hours away. Unlike many fans that were still hustling through the Cincinnati/Northern Kentucky and Louisville International airports, my Derby weekend was already made and the celebrating could begin an entire day early.

Paying a humongous $96.20 to win, the daughter of Lemon Drop Kid became the biggest upset in Oaks history, and I was one of the proud owners of a $7,125 pick-four ticket. It was a sharp reminder of how the Friday before the big dance, Oaks Day, has evolved as a day of optimum betting opportunities.

In recent years, Oaks Day has increased dramatically in popularity; the attendance has soared to well over 100,000 on-track, and there has been an average of nearly $10 million bet on the Oaks alone and another $20 million on the remainder of the card. What this means for horseplayers is that while Derby Day itself offers a saturated betting pool with many wagering opportunities, Oaks Day can be nearly as lucrative. A quick review of result charts from Oaks Day 2007 will hammer this point home.

FIRST RACE
Churchill
MAY 4, 2007

1 MILE. (1.33^{2}) ALLOWANCE OPTIONAL CLAIMING . Purse $55,000 (includes $9,900 KTDF – KY TB Devt Fund) FOR THREE YEAR OLDS AND UPWARD WHICH HAVE NEVER WON THREE RACES OTHER THAN MAIDEN, CLAIMING, STARTER, OR STATE BRED OR WHICH HAVE NEVER WON FOUR RACES OR CLAIMING PRICE $80,000. Three Year Olds, 118 lbs.; Older, 124 lbs. Non-winners Of $25,800 Twice At AMile Or Over Since November 1 Allowed 2 lbs. $22,800 twice at a mile or over in 2007 Allowed 4 lbs. (Races where entered for $62,500 or less not considered in allowances). (Rainy. 63.)

Value of Race: $47,080 Winner $27,962; second $11,000; third $4,510; fourth $2,255; fifth $1,353. Mutuel Pool $197,195.00 Exacta Pool $149,959.00 Trifecta Pool $96,038.00 Superfecta Pool $22,003.00

Last Raced	Horse	M/Eqt.	A.	Wt	PP	St	¼	½	¾	Str	Fin	Jockey	Cl'g Pr	Odds $1
12Apr07 ^{10}OP^{8}	Chippewa Trail	L b	6	120	1	7	$3^{1½}$	$1^{½}$	$1^{1½}$	$2^{1½}$	$1^{½}$	Guidry M	80000	5.40
13Apr07 ^{9}OP^{1}	Copy My Notes	L b	5	120	4	6	6^{4}	$3^{½}$	$3^{1½}$	1^{hd}	$2^{½}$	Borel C H		5.30
14Apr07 ^{7}Kee^{5}	Nar	L b	4	120	2	4	$1^{½}$	$2^{2½}$	2^{hd}	3^{2}	$3^{¾}$	Nakatani C S		4.10
24Mar07 ^{8}Haw^{1}	I'm Waiting for U	L b	4	120	6	2	7	7	7	$5^{1½}$	$4^{2½}$	Hernandez B J Jr	80000	13.30
24Mar07 ^{9}FG^{7}	Thunder Mission	L b	5	120	5	3	$5^{½}$	5^{2}	$4^{½}$	4^{1}	$5^{¾}$	Albarado R J	80000	2.20
29Mar07 ^{8}TP^{2}	Skippy Due	L b	5	120	3	5	4^{hd}	6^{4}	6^{1}	6^{1}	$6^{3¼}$	McKee J		8.00
6Aug06 ^{12}Mth^{8}	Deputy Glitters	L	4	120	7	1	2^{1}	$4^{1½}$	5^{4}	7	7	Bridgmohan S X		4.20

OFF AT 11:01 Start Good . Won driving. Track sloppy.

TIME :23, :45^{4}, 1:10, 1:22^{3}, 1:36^{2} (:23.15, :45.80, 1:10.04, 1:22.76, 1:36.46)

$2 Mutuel Prices:				
	1 – CHIPPEWA TRAIL	12.80	6.60	4.40
	5 – COPY MY NOTES		5.80	3.80
	3 – NAR			3.60

$2 EXACTA 1–5 PAID $68.00 $2 TRIFECTA 1–5–3 PAID $373.80
$2 SUPERFECTA 1–5–3–7 PAID $2,374.20

B. g, (Mar), by General Royal – Delight U. S. A. , by Quiet American . Trainer Lukas D Wayne. Bred by Mrs Stacy Mitchell & Briland Farm (Ky).

SECOND RACE
Churchill
MAY 4, 2007

1$\frac{1}{16}$ MILES. (1.41^{3}) MAIDEN SPECIAL WEIGHT . Purse $48,000 (includes $8,600 KTDF – KY TB Devt Fund) FOR MAIDENS, FILLIES AND MARES THREE YEARS OLD AND UPWARD. Three Year Olds, 118 lbs.; Older, 124 lbs. (Preference To Horses That Have Not Started For Less Than $30,000).

Value of Race: $46,280 Winner $30,018; second $7,880; third $4,800; fourth $2,400; fifth $1,182. Mutuel Pool $332,656.00 Exacta Pool $274,405.00 Trifecta Pool $200,782.00 Superfecta Pool $68,569.00

Last Raced	Horse	M/Eqt.	A.	Wt	PP	St	¼	½	¾	Str	Fin	Jockey	Cl'g Pr	Odds $1
11Apr07 ^{1}Kee^{4}	Le Peaks	L b	5	124	6	10	11	11	7^{hd}	$3^{½}$	$1^{2¾}$	Borel C H		25.00
11Apr07 ^{5}Kee^{8}	New York Dixie	L	3	118	3	9	$10^{4½}$	7^{2}	5^{3}	4^{3}	$2^{5¼}$	McKee J		8.40
11Apr07 ^{1}Kee^{3}	Artistic Escape	L	4	124	4	7	7^{1}	6^{1}	4^{1}	5^{7}	$3^{¾}$	Prado E S		8.70
11Apr07 ^{5}Kee^{7}	Sarah's Prize	L b	3	118	7	3	$2^{1½}$	$2^{3½}$	2^{5}	2^{2}	4^{nk}	Velazquez J R		1.60
15Mar07 ^{7}FG^{6}	Idoitmyway	L	3	118	5	2	$1^{1½}$	$1^{3½}$	$1^{2½}$	1^{1}	$5^{5¼}$	Bejarano R		7.60
8Feb07 ^{7}FG^{3}	Missamerica Bertie	L b	3	118	1	4	5^{hd}	$4^{1½}$	8^{3}	7^{2}	$6^{2½}$	Gomez G K		6.50
24Mar07 ^{12}TP^{6}	Lukes Brown Girl	L	3	118	2	8	8^{hd}	$9^{1½}$	9^{3}	9^{6}	7^{nk}	Martinez W		29.20
12Apr07 ^{4}Kee^{5}	Lady Attack	L	3	118	10	5	6^{2}	8^{2}	6^{hd}	$6^{½}$	8^{7}	Albarado R J		a- 7.70
11Apr07 ^{5}Kee^{4}	Matchless Moment	L	3	120	8	6	3^{1}	3^{2}	$3^{½}$	$8^{½}$	9^{3}	Nakatani C S		6.70
14Apr07 ^{5}Kee^{8}	Etched in Gold	L f	3	118	9	11	$9^{3½}$	10^{3}	10^{1}	10^{8}	$10^{18¼}$	Leparoux J R		a- 7.70
4Aug06 ^{10}ElP^{2}	Miss Abita	L b	3	118	11	1	$4^{2½}$	$5^{1½}$	11	11	11	Lanerie C J		19.10

a–Coupled: Lady Attack and Etched in Gold.

OFF AT 11:31 Start Good For All But ARTISTIC ESCAPE. Won driving. Track sloppy.

TIME :22^{4}, :46, 1:12, 1:40^{2}, 1:47^{2} (:22.88, :46.12, 1:12.01, 1:40.45, 1:47.59)

$2 Mutuel Prices:				
	7 – LE PEAKS	52.00	20.60	9.20
	4 – NEW YORK DIXIE		8.80	5.80
	5 – ARTISTIC ESCAPE			6.80

$2 EXACTA 7–4 PAID $493.40 $2 TRIFECTA 7–4–5 PAID $2,990.40
$2 SUPERFECTA 7–4–5–8 PAID $12,314.00

Dk. b or br. m, (Apr), by Peaks and Valleys – Flying Clear , by Cryptoclearance . Trainer Moore John. Bred by Ruth Fitzgerald (Ky).

THIRD RACE
Churchill
MAY 4, 2007

$1\frac{1}{16}$ MILES. (1.41³) ALLOWANCE . Purse $50,000 (includes $9,000 KTDF – KY TB Devt Fund) FOR THREE YEAR OLDS AND UPWARD WHICH HAVE NEVER WON A RACE OTHER THAN MAIDEN, CLAIMING OR STARTER OR WHICH HAVE NEVER WON TWO RACES. Three Year Olds, 118 lbs.; Older, 124 lbs. Non–winners Of $22,800 Over A Mile Since March 4 Allowed 2 lbs. $19,200 Over A Mile Since Then Allowed 4 lbs. (Races where entered for $30,000 or less not considered in allowances).

Value of Race: $50,000 Winner $31,270; second $10,000; third $5,000; fourth $2,500; fifth $1,230. Mutuel Pool $524,731.00 Exacta Pool $430,897.00 Trifecta Pool $327,684.00 Superfecta Pool $106,159.00

Last Raced	Horse	M/Eqt.	A.	Wt	PP	St	¼	½	¾	Str	Fin	Jockey	Cl'g Pr	Odds $1
26Feb07 8FG⁵	Don't Fret	L	4	120	6	11	11	11	9¹	21½	12¾	Borel C H		12.70
6Apr07 10Kee¹	True Competitor	L	3	118	4	3	3hd	3hd	31	32	2½	Prado E S		4.90
8Apr07 4GP³	Pennant Contender	L b	5	120	2	6	11	1½	1hd	11	3²	Nakatani C S		7.80
3Mar07 5GP⁷	Roman's Run	L	3	114	8	2	5hd	8¹	4½	42	47	Bejarano R		8.30
7Apr07 1SA¹	Pavarotti	L	3	114	11	7	8hd	10²	11	6¹	5¾	Gomez G K		2.30
6Apr07 4Kee⁶	Best Years	L b	4	120	7	8	7¹	6½	81½	8¹	6¾	Albarado R J		8.50
14Apr07 8OP²	Ifonlyjohnny	L b	3	116	1	10	9hd	9²½	10½	92½	7¾	Fires E		20.80
15Apr07 7Kee²	Shone	L b	4	120	9	9	104½	7hd	71½	7½	8½	Castro E		5.70
24Mar07 9GP⁶	Olympic	L b	5	120	10	5	4¹	21½	2²	5³	9⁶	Espinoza V		16.20
31Mar07 8OP²	Instant Messenger	L bf	4	120	3	1	6½	5hd	5½	101½	101	Desormeaux K J		25.70
11Mar07 3GP³	Prospect Begonia	L b	3	111	5	4	2¹	4½	6½	11	11	Leparoux J R		26.80

OFF AT 12:06 Start Good . Won driving. Track sloppy.

TIME :23³, :47³, 1:12², 1:38¹, 1:44⁴ (:23.70, :47.63, 1:12.51, 1:38.37, 1:44.96)

$2 Mutuel Prices:

7 – DON'T FRET	27.40	10.20	5.60
5 – TRUE COMPETITOR		6.00	3.80
3 – PENNANT CONTENDER			5.60

$2 EXACTA 7–5 PAID $206.80 $2 TRIFECTA 7–5–3 PAID $1,599.20
$2 SUPERFECTA 7–5–3–9 PAID $28,635.20

Gr/ro. c, (Mar), by El Prado–Ire – Round Robin , by Mt. Livermore . Trainer Margolis Steve. Bred by Bertram W Klein & Reklein Stables (Ky).

FOURTH RACE
Churchill
MAY 4, 2007

$1\frac{1}{16}$ MILES. (1.41³) 4TH RUNNING OF THE ALYSHEBA. Grade III. Purse $100,000 FOR THREE YEAR OLDS AND UPWARD. By subscription of $100 each on or before April 11, 2007 or by Supplementary Nomination of $5,000 at time of entry. $500 to pass the entry box; $500 additional to start, with $100,000 added. After payment of 1% to all owners of horses finishing sixth through last, 62% of the remaining purse shall be paid to the owner of the winner, 20% to second, 10% to third, 5% to fourth and 3% to fifth. Three–year–olds 117 lbs.; Older 124 lbs. Non–winners of a Grade I or II stakes at mile or over since September 1 allowed 2 lbs.; $60,000 twice at a mile or over since October 6, 4 lbs.; $60,000 at a mile or over in 2007, 6 lbs. The maximum number of starters for the Alysheba will be limited to fourteen (14). If more than fourteen (14) entries pass the entry box preference will be given to graded stakes winners, then highest 2006–2007 earnings. Any horse excluded from running because of the aforementioned preference shall be refunded the entry fee and supplementary nomination fee if applicable. Starters to be named through the entry box at the usual time of closing. All supplementary nominations will be required to pay entry and starting fees if they participate. Trophy to winning owner.

Value of Race: $112,300 Winner $68,236; second $22,010; third $11,005; fourth $5,502; fifth $3,301; sixth $1,123; seventh $1,123. Mutuel Pool $739,258.00 Exacta Pool $512,789.00 Trifecta Pool $371,149.00 Superfecta Pool $115,232.00

Last Raced	Horse	M/Eqt.	A.	Wt	PP	St	¼	½	¾	Str	Fin	Jockey	Cl'g Pr	Odds $1
24Nov06 11CD⁶	Wanderin Boy	L	6	124	2	3	1¹	11½	1½	1²	14¼	Nakatani C S		2.90
3Mar07 9GP¹	Half Ours	L	4	118	6	1	23½	2²	22½	2²	21½	Velazquez J R		2.00
6Apr07 8Kee⁴	Student Council	L	5	120	5	6	3½	3hd	32	3⁴	3⁸	Albarado R J		6.90
14Apr07 4Kee²	Perfect Drift	L b	8	118	1	7	7	7	6¹	41½	4³	Gomez G K		4.40
7Apr07 10OP²	Brother Bobby	L	4	118	4	5	5½	5½	4hd	52½	5nk	Elliott S		5.20
7Apr07 10OP⁶	Smokeyjonessutton	L	4	118	7	4	6³	61½	7	6³	69¼	Leparoux J R		11.20
3Mar07 6GP⁶	Summer Book	L b	6	118	3	2	4²	41½	5²	7	7	Guidry M		16.80

OFF AT 12:44 Start Good . Won driving. Track sloppy.

TIME :23³, :48, 1:12⁴, 1:37, 1:43² (:23.71, :48.09, 1:12.86, 1:37.04, 1:43.45)

$2 Mutuel Prices:

2 – WANDERIN BOY	7.80	4.00	3.40
6 – HALF OURS		3.80	3.20
5 – STUDENT COUNCIL			3.60

$2 EXACTA 2–6 PAID $23.40 $2 TRIFECTA 2–6–5 PAID $137.60
$2 SUPERFECTA 2–6–5–1 PAID $302.80

Ch. h, (Apr), by Seeking the Gold – Vid Kid , by Pleasant Colony . Trainer Zito Nicholas P. Bred by Arthur B Hancock III (Ky).

FIFTH RACE
1 $\frac{1}{16}$ MILES. (Turf) (1.40⁴) 23RD RUNNING OF THE EDGEWOOD. Purse $150,000 FOR FILLIES, THREE YEARS OLD.

Churchill
MAY 4, 2007

Value of Race: $171,150 Winner $102,929; second $33,207; third $16,601; fourth $8,300; fifth $4,980; sixth $1,711; seventh $1,711; eighth $1,711. Mutuel Pool $896,051.00 Exacta Pool $657,398.00 Trifecta Pool $484,263.00 Superfecta Pool $152,917.00

Last Raced	Horse	M/Eqt. A. Wt	PP	St	$\frac{1}{4}$	$\frac{1}{2}$	$\frac{3}{4}$	Str	Fin	Jockey	Cl'g Pr	Odds $1
22Apr07 8Kee6	Swingit	L b 3 121	7	7	8	8	7½	3½	1hd	Hernandez B J Jr		7.90
24Feb07 11TP5	Luna Dorada	L 3 117	6	6	6½	6½	5hd	2hd	22½	Bejarano R		26.30
22Apr07 8Kee8	Good Mood-Ire	L 3 117	8	8	7hd	7½	8	61	31¾	Leparoux J R		2.70
25Mar07 4FG1	Moonee Ponds	L 3 121	4	2	21½	23	1hd	11	41½	Theriot H J II		1.60
11Apr07 4Kee3	Nola Star	L 3 117	5	1	52	4½	41½	51	5¾	Desormeaux K J		5.20
11Apr07 7Kee4	Queen of the Ridge	L b 3 117	2	4	1½	11½	23½	42	6½	Martinez W		28.80
14Apr07 10OP2	Nice Inheritance	L 3 117	3	3	4hd	51½	61½	7½	71	Albarado R J		6.00
2Mar07 7GP3	Striking Tomisue	L b 3 120	1	5	33	32	3½	8	8	Nakatani C S		15.30

OFF AT 1:27 Start Good. Won driving. Course yielding.

TIME :23⁴, :48³, 1:11¹, 1:37⁴, 1:43⁴ (:23.82, :48.70, 1:11.26, 1:37.85, 1:43.99)

$2 Mutuel Prices:	8 – SWINGIT	17.80	7.80	4.80
	7 – LUNA DORADA		20.20	8.00
	9 – GOOD MOOD-IRE			3.40

$2 EXACTA 8–7 PAID $442.40 $2 TRIFECTA 8–7–9 PAID $1,899.60
$2 SUPERFECTA 8–7–9–5 PAID $6,670.20

B. f, (Apr), by Victory Gallop – Free Ransom, by Our Native. Trainer Wiggins Hal R. Bred by Robert V Hovelson (Ky).

SIXTH RACE
6 FURLONGS. (1.07²) ALLOWANCE. Purse $50,000 (includes $9,000 KTDF – KY TB Devt Fund) FOR FILLIES THREE YEARS OLD WHICH HAVE NEVER WON A RACE OTHER THAN MAIDEN, CLAIMING OR STARTER OR WHICH HAVE NEVER WON TWO RACES. Weight, 123 lbs. Non-winners Of $22,800 Since March 4 Allowed 3 lbs. $19,200 since then Allowed 5 lbs. (Races Where Entered For $30,000 Or Less Not Considered In Allowances.)

Churchill
MAY 4, 2007

Value of Race: $50,000 Winner $31,270; second $10,000; third $5,000; fourth $2,500; fifth $1,230. Mutuel Pool $1,294,868.00 Exacta Pool $918,855.00 Trifecta Pool $690,297.00 Superfecta Pool $234,847.00

Last Raced	Horse	M/Eqt. A. Wt	PP	St	$\frac{1}{4}$	$\frac{1}{2}$	Str	Fin	Jockey	Cl'g Pr	Odds $1
13Apr07 5GP6	Tora	L 3 118	7	2	31	35½	33	1hd	Prado E S		7.90
6Apr07 7Kee5	Gem Sleuth	L 3 118	2	4	7hd	7½	42	21¾	Leparoux J R		14.00
23Sep06 8Bel2	Featherbed	L 3 118	1	3	1½	21½	1hd	31¼	Velazquez J R		3.50
12Nov06 8Aqu2	Meredith Bee	L 3 118	9	9	9³	81	5hd	41¼	Gomez G K		13.70
10Mar07 9TP1	Angels' Share	L 3 118	8	11	12	111	71	5½	Troilo W D		29.20
1Jly06 9Hol4	Thru n' Thru	L b 3 118	10	1	21	1½	21½	6½	Espinoza V		7.10
18Mar07 9GP2	Early Vintage	L 3 118	5	12	8½	41½	63	73¾	Bejarano R		8.30
30Mar07 8OP2	Lady Takum	L 3 118	12	10	11⁵	10⁵	96	85¾	Bridgmohan S X		23.40
22Mar07 8FG2	Graeme Six	L 3 118	6	7	51	51½	8hd	99½	Lanerie C J		2.50
18Mar07 7GP3	Lilly Carson	L 3 118	11	8	61½	91	113	101¼	Albarado R J		12.90
11Mar07 8FG1	Beyond Infinity	L 3 123	4	6	4hd	6hd	102	111	Nakatani C S		23.00
6Apr07 7Kee8	Grecourt Gates	L 3 118	3	5	10hd	12	12	12	Melancon L		34.60

OFF AT 2:12 Start Good For All But EARLY VINTAGE. Won driving. Track sloppy.

TIME :21², :44⁴, :57³, 1:11 (:21.52, :44.99, :57.61, 1:11.17)

	7 – TORA	17.80	8.20	5.60
$2 Mutuel Prices:	2 – GEM SLEUTH		12.80	7.60
	1 – FEATHERBED			4.20

$2 EXACTA 7–2 PAID $207.20 $2 TRIFECTA 7–2–1 PAID $1,192.80
$2 SUPERFECTA 7–2–1–9 PAID $14,059.20

Dk. b or br. f, (Jan), by El Corredor – Everyone's Honour, by Mt. Livermore. Trainer Dutrow Richard E Jr. Bred by Heiligbrodt Racing Stable (Ky).

SEVENTH RACE
Churchill
MAY 4, 2007

5 FURLONGS. (Turf) (.55²) 13TH RUNNING OF THE AEGON TURF SPRINT. Grade III. Purse $150,000 FOR THREE-YEAR-OLDS AND UPWARD.

Value of Race: $169,050 Winner $101,671; second $32,795; third $16,397; fourth $8,198; fifth $4,919; sixth $1,690; seventh $1,690; eighth $1,690. Mutuel Pool $1,163,089.00 Exacta Pool $723,469.00 Trifecta Pool $524,110.00 Superfecta Pool $166,309.00

Last Raced	Horse	M/Eqt.	A.	Wt	PP	St	$\frac{3}{16}$	$\frac{3}{8}$	Str	Fin	Jockey	Cl'g Pr	Odds $1
24Mar07 9FG4	Gaff	L	5	121	4	3	4hd	3hd	3²	11¼	Velazquez J R		3.80
15Mar07 7SA1	Ellwood and Jake	L	4	118	5	7	6½	6hd	4½	2¾	Gomez G K		5.50
15Apr07 8Kee2	Congo King	L	4	118	1	5	5½	52½	5¹	31¼	Leparoux J R		6.20
24Mar07 4SA2	Roi Charmant	L b	6	118	6	8	8	7²	7²	4hd	Flores D R		7.80
15Apr07 8Kee1	The Nth Degree	L f	6	121	2	4	3½	41½	6¹	52½	Castro E		8.40
3Nov06 9CD1	Unbridled Sidney	L	6	117	3	1	1½	1hd	1hd	6½	Albarado R J		2.00
7Apr07 9Hou2	Chief What It Is	L b	4	118	7	2	23½	2³	2hd	7hd	Theriot H J II		16.60
15Apr07 8Kee3	Sgt. Bert	L	6	118	8	6	7hd	8	8	8	Bejarano R		10.20

OFF AT 3:04 Start Good. Won driving. Course yielding.

TIME :21⁴, :45, :56⁴ (:21.88, :45.12, :56.84)

$2 Mutuel Prices:

6 – GAFF	9.60	5.00	3.60
7 – ELLWOOD AND JAKE		5.80	3.80
1 – CONGO KING			5.00

$2 EXACTA 6-7 PAID $55.40 $2 TRIFECTA 6-7-1 PAID $360.20
$2 SUPERFECTA 6-7-1-8 PAID $1,973.00

B. h, (Mar), by Maria's Mon – Ionlyhaveeyesforu, by Tunerup. Trainer Asmussen Steven M. Bred by Earle Irving Mack (Ky).

EIGHTH RACE
Churchill
MAY 4, 2007

1¹⁄₁₆ MILES. (1.41³) 22ND RUNNING OF THE LOUISVILLE BREEDERS' CUP. Grade II. Purse $300,000 (includes $100,000 BC – Breeders' Cup) FOR FILLIES AND MARES THREE YEARS OLD AND UPWARD.

Value of Race: $305,197 Winner $202,069; second $45,183; third $32,591; fourth $16,295; fifth $6,777; sixth $2,282. Mutuel Pool $1,464,127.00 Exacta Pool $889,323.00 Trifecta Pool $571,572.00 Superfecta Pool $159,946.00

Last Raced	Horse	M/Eqt.	A.	Wt	PP	St	¼	½	¾	Str	Fin	Jockey	Cl'g Pr	Odds $1
11Apr07 9OP3	Fiery Pursuit	L b	4	118	5	1	11½	1¹	1½	11½	1hd	Borel C H		11.80
18Apr07 8Kee1	Asi Siempre	L b	5	122	1	5	51½	51½	4hd	2hd	2¾	Gomez G K		2.50
7Apr07 8OP4	Baghdaria	L	4	118	2	4	3²	3²	3¹	4³	31¾	Bejarano R		6.80
31Mar07 8Aqu1	Indian Vale	L	5	120	4	2	2²	2²	21½	3½	4²	Velazquez J R		1.30
31Mar07 2DeD1	Delicate Dynamite	L	4	120	6	3	4²	4½	5³	53½	55½	Albarado R J		3.90
7Apr07 8OP7	Lemons Forever	L	4	118	3	6	6	6	6	6	6	Guidry M		10.60

OFF AT 3:55 Start Good. Won driving. Track sloppy.

TIME :23³, :47⁴, 1:12, 1:37, 1:44 (:23.77, :47.84, 1:12.07, 1:37.18, 1:44.11)

$2 Mutuel Prices:

5 – FIERY PURSUIT	25.60	7.80	4.40
1 – ASI SIEMPRE		4.00	3.00
2 – BAGHDARIA			4.60

$2 EXACTA 5-1 PAID $112.00 $2 TRIFECTA 5-1-2 PAID $435.80
$2 SUPERFECTA 5-1-2-4 PAID $1,155.60

Ch. f, (Jan), by Carson City – Engaging, by Private Account. Trainer Lukas D Wayne. Bred by Overbrook Farm (Ky).

NINTH RACE
Churchill
MAY 4, 2007

$1\frac{1}{16}$ MILES. (Turf) (1.40^{4}) 16TH RUNNING OF THE CROWN ROYAL AMERICAN TURF. Grade III. Purse $150,000 FOR THREE-YEAR-OLDS.

Value of Race: $188,700 Winner $111,146; second $35,853; third $17,926; fourth $8,963; fifth $5,377; sixth $1,887; seventh $1,887; eighth $1,887; ninth $1,887; tenth $1,887. Mutuel Pool $1,637,020.00 Exacta Pool $953,651.00 Trifecta Pool $731,313.00 Superfecta Pool $259,145.00

Last Raced	Horse	M/Eqt.	A.	Wt	PP	St	¼	½	¾	Str	Fin	Jockey	Cl'g Pr	Odds $1
24Mar07 ^{7}GP^{1}	Duveen	L	3	123	4	3	2^{1}	2^{1}	$2^{\frac{1}{2}}$	1^{1}	$1^{\frac{1}{2}}$	Guidry M		4.60
16Mar07 ^{7}SA^{1}	Whatsthescript-Ire	L	3	123	2	5	5^{1}	4^{1}	6^{1}	4^{2}	$2^{\frac{1}{2}}$	Enriquez I D		3.60
24Mar07 ^{6}FG^{1}	Jazz Quest	L	3	121	3	6	$1^{\frac{1}{2}}$	1^{1}	$1^{\frac{1}{2}}$	2^{1}	$3^{\frac{1}{2}}$	Leparoux J R		17.30
6Apr07 ^{9}Kee^{1}	Marcavelly	L	3	123	5	2	3^{hd}	$3^{\frac{1}{2}}$	$3^{\frac{1}{2}}$	3^{2}	4no	Prado E S		2.90
12Apr07 ^{5}Kee^{1}	Distorted Reality	L b	3	117	8	8	$7^{2\frac{1}{2}}$	6^{hd}	7^{1}	5^{hd}	5^{1}	Velazquez J R		5.30
26Mar07 ^{5}GP^{1}	Top Cross	L	3	117	7	1	$8^{2\frac{1}{2}}$	$8^{\frac{1}{2}}$	$8^{1\frac{1}{2}}$	6^{hd}	$6^{2\frac{1}{2}}$	Gomez G K		13.80
31Mar07 ^{11}GP^{7}	Birdbirdistheword	L b	3	117	6	7	6^{hd}	5^{hd}	$4^{\frac{1}{2}}$	8^{2}	7^{nk}	Albarado R J		6.60
25Apr07 ^{6}Kee^{1}	Royal War Academy	L	3	117	1	4	4^{hd}	7^{1}	5^{hd}	$7^{\frac{1}{2}}$	8^{nk}	Elliott S		40.00
14Apr07 ^{11}OP^{4}	Delightful Kiss	L f	3	118	9	9	$9^{5\frac{1}{2}}$	$9^{2\frac{1}{2}}$	9^{4}	$9^{1\frac{1}{2}}$	9^{nk}	Theriot H J II		18.40
6Apr07 ^{9}Kee^{3}	Cobrador	L b	3	117	10	10	10	10	10	10	10	Borel C H		17.50

OFF AT 4:48 Start Good. Won driving. Course yielding.

TIME :24^{3}, :50, 1:14^{4}, 1:38, 1:44 (:24.70, :50.09, 1:14.98, 1:38.06, 1:44.03)

$2 Mutuel Prices:				
	4 – DUVEEN	11.20	6.20	5.20
	2 – WHATSTHESCRIPT-IRE		5.40	4.20
	3 – JAZZ QUEST			7.40

$2 EXACTA 4–2 PAID $50.60 $2 TRIFECTA 4–2–3 PAID $622.40
$2 SUPERFECTA 4–2–3–5 PAID $2,176.80

Dk. b or br. c, (Apr), by Horse Chestnut–SAf – Casanova Storm, by Storm Cat. Trainer Romans Dale. Bred by Richard Brodie Robert Scanlon & James Buckley (Ky).

TENTH RACE
Churchill
MAY 4, 2007

1⅛ MILES. (1.47^{1}) 133RD RUNNING OF THE KENTUCKY OAKS. Grade I. Purse $500,000 FILLIES, THREE YEARS OLD.

Value of Race: $589,200 Winner $332,428; second $107,234; third $53,617; fourth $26,808; fifth $16,085; sixth $5,892; seventh $5,892; eighth $5,892; ninth $5,892; tenth $5,892; eleventh $5,892; twelfth $5,892; thirteenth $5,892; fourteenth $5,892. Mutuel Pool $3,711,167.00 Exacta Pool $2,068,072.00 Trifecta Pool $1,830,669.00 Superfecta Pool $713,167.00

Last Raced	Horse	M/Eqt.	A.	Wt	PP	St	¼	½	¾	Str	Fin	Jockey	Cl'g Pr	Odds $1
11Mar07 ^{9}SA^{1}	Rags to Riches	L	3	121	11	7	4^{hd}	5^{hd}	$5^{1\frac{1}{2}}$	1^{2}	$1^{4\frac{1}{4}}$	Gomez G K		1.50
7Apr07 ^{9}Kee^{2}	Octave	L	3	121	4	2	$7^{\frac{1}{2}}$	$7^{\frac{1}{2}}$	6^{hd}	$2^{\frac{1}{2}}$	$2^{3\frac{1}{2}}$	Velazquez J R		6.40
6Apr07 ^{9}OP^{1}	High Heels	L	3	121	3	8	10^{2}	9^{hd}	8^{hd}	4^{hd}	$3^{3\frac{1}{4}}$	Johnson J M		6.20
7Apr07 ^{9}Kee^{3}	Dawn After Dawn	L	3	121	1	3	12^{3}	$12^{3\frac{1}{2}}$	10^{hd}	$5^{\frac{1}{2}}$	4^{2}	Albarado R J		34.00
7Apr07 ^{9}Kee^{5}	Mistical Plan	L	3	121	13	6	$2^{\frac{1}{2}}$	$2^{1\frac{1}{2}}$	2^{1}	3^{1}	$5^{3\frac{3}{4}}$	Flores D R		24.00
25Feb07 ^{7}GP^{2}	Dreaming of Anna	L	3	121	7	4	$1^{\frac{1}{2}}$	1^{hd}	$1^{\frac{1}{2}}$	6^{4}	$6^{\frac{1}{2}}$	Douglas R R		5.80
18Mar07 ^{8}Sun^{1}	Tough Tiz's Sis	L b	3	121	9	13	9^{hd}	10^{hd}	$7^{1\frac{1}{2}}$	7^{2}	$7^{2\frac{1}{2}}$	Espinoza V		23.30
17Mar07 ^{10}Tam^{4}	Autobahn Girl	L	3	121	10	11	$8^{1\frac{1}{2}}$	8^{1}	9^{1}	9^{2}	8^{nk}	Castro E		16.00
6Apr07 ^{9}OP^{2}	Cotton Blossom	L	3	121	5	1	3^{hd}	$4^{\frac{1}{2}}$	4^{hd}	8^{2}	$9^{2\frac{1}{4}}$	Prado E S		13.60
6Apr07 ^{9}OP^{4}	Swift Temper	L b	3	121	8	12	$11^{\frac{1}{2}}$	11^{2}	11^{3}	$10^{\frac{1}{2}}$	$10^{1\frac{1}{2}}$	Leparoux J R		40.00
6Apr07 ^{9}OP^{3}	Cash Included	L b	3	121	2	10	14	13^{4}	13	$11^{\frac{1}{2}}$	$11^{2\frac{1}{4}}$	Nakatani C S		39.60
24Mar07 ^{8}TP^{1}	Sealy Hill	L b	3	121	12	5	5^{1}	$3^{\frac{1}{2}}$	$3^{\frac{1}{2}}$	12^{12}	$12^{25\frac{1}{2}}$	Husbands P		40.70
7Apr07 ^{9}Kee^{4}	High Again	L	3	121	14	9	$6^{\frac{1}{2}}$	6^{1}	12^{2}	13	13	Velasquez C		21.50
7Apr07 ^{9}Kee^{6}	Grace Happens	L b	3	121	6	14	13^{hd}	14	—	—	—	Martinez W		42.10

OFF AT 5:47 Start Good. Won driving. Track muddy.

TIME :23^{1}, :47^{4}, 1:12^{3}, 1:37^{4}, 1:49^{4} (:23.25, :47.89, 1:12.69, 1:37.80, 1:49.99)

$2 Mutuel Prices:				
	11 – RAGS TO RICHES	5.00	3.80	2.80
	4 – OCTAVE		5.20	3.60
	3 – HIGH HEELS			3.60

$2 EXACTA 11–4 PAID $30.00 $2 TRIFECTA 11–4–3 PAID $131.00
$2 SUPERFECTA 11–4–3–1 PAID $1,830.60

Ch. f, (Feb), by A.P. Indy – Better Than Honour, by Deputy Minister. Trainer Pletcher Todd A. Bred by Skara Glen Stables (Ky).

ELEVENTH RACE
Churchill
MAY 4, 2007

7 FURLONGS. (1.20²) MAIDEN SPECIAL WEIGHT . Purse $48,000 (includes $8,600 KTDF – KY TB Devt Fund) FOR MAIDENS, THREE YEAR OLDS AND UPWARD. Three Year Olds, 118 lbs.; Older, 124 lbs. (Preference To Horses That Have Not Started For Less Than $30,000).

Value of Race: $45,850 Winner $30,018; second $7,880; third $4,800; fourth $1,970; fifth $1,182. Mutuel Pool $1,002,214.00 Exacta Pool $696,413.00 Trifecta Pool $582,735.00 Superfecta Pool $243,736.00

Last Raced	Horse	M/Eqt.	A.	Wt	PP	St	¼	½	Str	Fin	Jockey	Cl'g Pr	Odds $1
25Nov06 3CD4	Codio	L	3	118	5	4	3hd	24	14½	15½	Prado E S		2.10
	For Michael's Dad	L	3	118	6	5	5hd	5½	24	22¼	Gomez G K		3.80
11Nov06 10CD11	Mutadda	L b	3	118	9	6	7hd	7hd	42	31½	Martinez W		19.20
8Dec06 2WO4	Prized Native	L	3	118	1	10	6½1	6½1	65	45½	Bridgmohan S X		15.80
13Apr07 10Kee3	Sly	L b	3	118	10	7	93	83	5hd	51¾	Albarado R J		3.60
25Aug06 5ElP3	Rovic's Wealth	L bf	3	118	8	8	82	98	72	66¾	Troilo W D		36.60
13Apr07 6Kee5	Leveraged	L	3	118	4	3	45	31	89	72	Theriot H J II		11.00
	Garifine	L	3	118	2	2	11	1hd	3hd	85½	Velazquez J R		4.60
4Apr07 6TP8	Vilas County	L	3	118	7	9	10	10	94	99½	Leparoux J R		33.10
6Apr07 5Kee12	Ameliaislandmissle	L b	3	118	3	1	2½	41	10	10	McKee J		35.50

OFF AT 6:40 Start Good . Won driving. Track muddy.

TIME :224, :462, 1:104, 1:233 (:22.97, :46.45, 1:10.87, 1:23.69)

$2 Mutuel Prices:

6 – CODIO	6.20	3.40	2.80
7 – FOR MICHAEL'S DAD		4.80	3.80
11 – MUTADDA			6.80

$2 EXACTA 6–7 PAID $24.40 $2 TRIFECTA 6–7–11 PAID $354.20
$2 SUPERFECTA 6–7–11–1 PAID $2,897.00

B. c, (Mar), by Doneraile Court – The Church Lady , by Valid Wager . Trainer Asmussen Steven M. Bred by Fred Pace (Ky).

Following is a recap of the result charts from Oaks Day 2006. The 2006 edition did not offer as much value in the win pool as 2007, with a total of six winners paying less than 7–2. However, there was still plenty of value to be found for those players choosing to participate in intra-race and multi-race betting pools.

For example, even after eliminating the robust $12,000 and $89,000 Oaks trifecta and superfecta from the day's average, the remaining 10 races still managed a median trifecta of over $350 and a superfecta of roughly $2,200.

It becomes obvious that as with the Kentucky Derby, there is tremendous value on this particular afternoon, and it is extremely worthwhile to study the past performances as rigorously as you can, and as far in advance as possible.

The value lies in the fact that the uniformed public, as well as most handicappers, sports journalists, and other writers covering the event, have spent countless hours focusing *only* on the Triple Crown race while neglecting the other wonderful betting opportunities available pre-Derby and on both race-day undercards. These types of races offer plenty of low-hanging fruit with millions of dollars waiting to be disbursed to the savvy bettors who are smart and ambitious enough to capitalize on the weaknesses of their parimutuel rivals.

FIRST RACE
Churchill
MAY 5, 2006

5 FURLONGS. (.56²) MAIDEN SPECIAL WEIGHT . Purse $50,000 (includes $10,000 KTDF – Kentucky TB Devt Fund) FOR MAIDENS, FILLIES TWO YEARS OLD. Weight, 119 lbs. (Preference to horses that have not started for $30,000 or less). (Cloudy. 66.)

Value of Race: $43,500 Winner $24,800; second $10,000; third $5,000; fourth $2,500; fifth $1,200. Mutuel Pool $249,557.00 Exacta Pool $168,532.00 Trifecta Pool $93,296.00 Superfecta Pool $20,139.00

Last Raced	Horse	M/Eqt.	A.	Wt	PP	St	$\frac{3}{16}$	$\frac{3}{8}$	Str	Fin	Jockey	Odds $1
	Alotofappeal	L	2	119	5	4	1hd	1hd	1hd	1no	Gomez G K	2.80
	Change Up	L	2	119	4	5	2¹	2¹½	22½	22¾	Castanon J L	2.60
13Apr06 3Kee4	Natalicat	L	2	119	6	8	6³	6⁶	41½	31	Douglas R R	15.20
13Apr06 3Kee3	Expertise	L	2	119	7	3	31½	3½	31½	44½	Jacinto J	4.70
	Gold Minx	L	2	119	3	7	8	8	6²	53½	McKee J	13.70
13Apr06 3Kee5	Distinctive Gold	L b	2	119	8	2	4hd	42½	55	67	Albarado R J	22.20
20Apr06 4Kee7	Crimson Whisper	L	2	119	2	6	7¹	7hd	8	71	Martinez W	34.50
	Lunarlady	L	2	119	1	1	5⁴	5¹	7⁴	8	Bridgmohan S X	2.50

OFF AT 11:05 Start Good. Won driving. Track fast.
TIME :22, :45², :57⁴ (:22.03, :45.44, :57.96)

$2 Mutuel Prices:

7 – ALOTOFAPPEAL	7.60	4.20	3.00
6 – CHANGE UP		3.80	3.00
8 – NATALICAT			5.40

$2 EXACTA 7–6 PAID $24.80 $2 TRIFECTA 7–6–8 PAID $350.20
$2 SUPERFECTA 7–6–8–9 PAID $1,051.20

B. f, (Mar), by Trippi – Argos Appeal , by World Appeal . Trainer Pletcher Todd A. Bred by Diane Dudley (Fla).

SECOND RACE
Churchill
MAY 5, 2006

6 FURLONGS. (1.07²) ALLOWANCE . Purse $54,000 (includes $11,000 KTDF – Kentucky TB Devt Fund) FOR FILLIES AND MARES THREE YEARS OLD AND UPWARD WHICH HAVE NEVER WON A RACE OTHER THAN MAIDEN, CLAIMING OR STARTER OR WHICH HAVE NEVER WON TWO RACES. Three Year Olds, 118 lbs.; Older, 124 lbs. Non–winners of a race since April 1 Allowed 2 lbs. A race since March 1 Allowed 4 lbs. (Races where entered for $30,000 or less not considered).

Value of Race: $53,450 Winner $33,810; second $10,800; third $5,400; fourth $2,150; fifth $1,290. Mutuel Pool $326,492.00 Exacta Pool $274,936.00 Trifecta Pool $185,447.00 Superfecta Pool $50,897.00

Last Raced	Horse	M/Eqt.	A.	Wt	PP	St	¼	½	Str	Fin	Jockey	Odds $1
9Nov05 8CD²	Naughty Is	L	4	120	2	5	4½	2½	1hd	12¼	Guidry M	2.10
24Mar06 9OP¹	Kathy's Lil Cat	L	4	122	3	4	51	3½	2hd	22	Albarado R J	3.10
21Dec05 9TP⁴	Sister Bay	L b	4	115	1	6	64	5½	42½	31¼	Leparoux J R⁵	3.70
13Apr06 9OP⁵	Lucky Jen	L bf	4	120	4	1	11	1hd	33½	41¼	Borel C H	9.60
27Apr06 9Kee⁸	Sabbath Day Point	L	5	120	6	7	7	7	63	55¾	Johnson J M	13.50
11Mar06 9TP⁷	Shining Victory	L b	5	120	5	2	3½	4hd	5½	64	Douglas R R	13.90
12Apr06 5Kee¹	Impelling	L b	3	118	7	3	2½	64	7	7	Jacinto J	4.10

OFF AT 11:34 Start Good. Won driving. Track fast.

TIME :21³, :45¹, :57¹, 1:10 (:21.70, :45.25, :57.38, 1:10.00)

$2 Mutuel Prices:	2 – NAUGHTY IS	6.20	3.00	2.40
	3 – KATHY'S LIL CAT		3.60	2.80
	1 – SISTER BAY			3.00

$2 EXACTA 2–3 PAID $16.80 $2 TRIFECTA 2–3–1 PAID $51.40
$2 SUPERFECTA 2–3–1–4 PAID $267.40

Dk. b or br. f, (Apr), by Bianconi – Pledge , by Woodman . Trainer Smith Thomas V. Bred by Dinnaken Farm (Ky).

THIRD RACE
Churchill
MAY 5, 2006

1 1/16 MILES. (1.41¹) ALLOWANCE . Purse $54,000 (includes $11,000 KTDF – Kentucky TB Devt Fund) FOR FILLIES AND MARES THREE YEARS OLD AND UPWARD WHICH HAVE NEVER WON A RACE OTHER THAN MAIDEN, CLAIMING OR STARTER OR WHICH HAVE NEVER WON TWO RACES. Three Year Olds, 117 lbs.; Older, 124 lbs. Non–winners of a race at a mile or over since April 1 Allowed 2 lbs. Such a race since March 1 Allowed 4 lbs. (Races where entered for $30,000 or less not considered).

Value of Race: $54,000 Winner $33,810; second $10,800; third $5,400; fourth $2,700; fifth $1,290. Mutuel Pool $454,378.00 Exacta Pool $403,816.00 Trifecta Pool $273,548.00 Superfecta Pool $76,969.00

Last Raced	Horse	M/Eqt.	A.	Wt	PP	St	¼	½	¾	Str	Fin	Jockey	Odds $1
8Mar06 9OP⁵	Auntie Soph	L	5	120	5	3	4½	41	31½	31½	1hd	Bejarano R	6.70
21Apr06 8Kee⁴	Unkatzable	L b	3	116	1	4	11½	1hd	2½	2hd	2hd	Guidry M	3.80
9Apr06 7Kee⁶	Bootery	L	3	113	2	5	2½	31½	1hd	1hd	31¼	Castellano J J	6.10
15Apr06 11OP²	Shesanidem	L bf	3	117	4	1	31½	2½	41	43	43¼	Borel C H	5.00
25Mar06 3TP³	Enjoythe Afternoon	L	4	120	7	2	71½	72	7	7	5nk	Douglas R R	8.60
1Apr06 9TP²	Kickin' the Clouds	L	3	117	8	6	61½	62	62	5½	62¼	Lanerie C J	2.90
9Nov05 8CD⁸	Pacific Destiny	L b	4	120	3	8	5hd	5hd	5hd	6hd	7	Velasquez C	23.60
19Apr06 3Kee⁴	Valor Within	L b	4	115	6	7	8	8	—	—	—	Leparoux J R⁵	5.50

OFF AT 12:06 Start Good. Won driving. Track fast.

TIME :24³, :49², 1:14², 1:38¹, 1:44¹ (:24.67, :49.48, 1:14.53, 1:38.24, 1:44.32)

$2 Mutuel Prices:	5 – AUNTIE SOPH	15.40	7.60	6.00
	1A – UNKATZABLE		5.80	4.60
	2 – BOOTERY			6.40

$2 EXACTA 5–1 PAID $95.00 $2 TRIFECTA 5–1–2 PAID $769.60
$2 SUPERFECTA 5–1–2–4 PAID $7,863.80

Gr/ro. m, (Apr), by Valiant Nature – Martha Sophia , by Drone . Trainer Nicks Ralph E. Bred by Dr John A Chandler (Ky).

FOURTH RACE
Churchill
MAY 5, 2006

1 MILE. (1.33^2) ALLOWANCE. Purse $58,000 (includes $12,000 KTDF – Kentucky TB Devt Fund) FOR THREE YEAR OLDS AND UPWARD WHICH HAVE NEVER WON TWO RACES OTHER THAN MAIDEN, CLAIMING OR STARTER OR WHICH HAVE NEVER WON THREE RACES. Three Year Olds, 117 lbs.; Older, 124 lbs. Non-winners of a race at a mile or over since April 1 Allowed 2 lbs. Such a race since March 1 Allowed 4 lbs. (Races where entered for $30,000 or less not considered).

Value of Race: $56,800 Winner $36,320; second $11,600; third $4,600; fourth $2,900; fifth $1,380. Mutuel Pool $778,031.00 Exacta Pool $602,959.00 Trifecta Pool $477,617.00 Superfecta Pool $169,125.00

Last Raced	Horse	M/Eqt.	A.	Wt	PP	St	¼	½	¾	Str	Fin	Jockey	Odds $1
11Mar06 ^{3}GP^{1}	Venetian Sunset	L	4	122	7	3	1^{hd}	1^{hd}	$1^{1\frac{1}{2}}$	$1^{4\frac{1}{2}}$	$1^{7\frac{3}{4}}$	Gomez G K	0.70
18Mar06 ^{8}GP^{3}	Bank President	L	4	120	1	6	6^{1}	3^{hd}	$5^{\frac{1}{2}}$	3^{hd}	$2^{1\frac{1}{4}}$	Bejarano R	3.80
12Apr06 ^{4}Kee^{1}	Nar	L	3	113	6	2	$3^{\frac{1}{2}}$	5^{2}	4^{1}	5^{hd}	3^{hd}	Castellano J J	4.90
8Apr06 ^{12}OP^{8}	Prayer Service	L b	4	120	9	8	7^{1}	$7^{\frac{1}{2}}$	7^{4}	$6^{2\frac{1}{2}}$	4^{1}	McKee J	20.60
31Mar06 ^{10}TP^{1}	Nerinx	L b	4	120	5	1	5^{hd}	4^{hd}	3^{hd}	4^{hd}	$5^{1\frac{1}{2}}$	Velasquez C	18.40
4Mar06 ^{8}Hou^{6}	Rungius	L b	3	117	4	5	2^{1}	$2^{\frac{1}{2}}$	2^{1}	$2^{\frac{1}{2}}$	6no	Castanon J L	30.70
8Apr06 ^{5}Kee^{9}	Third Day	L b	5	113	3	7	$8^{2\frac{1}{2}}$	$8^{1\frac{1}{2}}$	9	8^{hd}	$7^{\frac{3}{4}}$	Toups R^{7}	40.90
15Apr06 ^{7}Haw^{1}	A Classic Aussie	L b	4	120	8	9	9	9	$8^{\frac{1}{2}}$	9	8^{2}	Guidry M	40.90
25Mar06 ^{9}TP^{4}	New Awakening	L	3	113	2	4	4^{hd}	$6^{2\frac{1}{2}}$	6^{1}	$7^{1\frac{1}{2}}$	9	Chavez C R	14.80

OFF AT 12:44 Start Good. Won driving. Track fast.

TIME $:22^2$, :45, $1:09^3$, $1:21^3$, $1:34^2$ (:22.42, :45.12, 1:09.62, 1:21.72, 1:34.46)

$2 Mutuel Prices:

7 – VENETIAN SUNSET	3.40	2.40	2.20
1 – BANK PRESIDENT		3.80	2.60
6 – NAR			2.60

$2 EXACTA 7–1 PAID $10.40 $2 TRIFECTA 7–1–6 PAID $27.00
$2 SUPERFECTA 7–1–6–9 PAID $195.00

Ch. c, (Apr), by Old Trieste – Shining Through, by Deputy Minister. Trainer Pletcher Todd A. Bred by Liberation Farm Trackside Farm & CHO LLC (Ky).

FIFTH RACE
Churchill
MAY 5, 2006

1$\frac{1}{16}$ MILES. (Turf) (1.40^3) 22ND RUNNING OF THE EDGEWOOD. Purse $100,000 FOR FILLIES, THREE YEARS OLD. By subscription of $100 each on or before April 8, 2006 or by Supplementary Nomination of $5,000 at time of entry. $500 to pass the entry box; $500 additional to start, with $100,000 added. After payment of 1% to all owners of horses finishing sixth through last, 62% of the remaining purse shall be paid to the owner of the winner, 20% to second, 10% to third, 5% to fourth and 3% to fifth. Weight 122 lbs. Non-winners of a sweepstakes on the turf allowed 2 lbs.; three races other than maiden or claiming, 4 lbs.; two races other than maiden or claiming, 6 lbs. If the race is moved to the main track after time of closing, a horse may be scratched for any reason at any time up to fifteen (15) minutes prior to post time for the race preceding this race or thereafter with a valid physical reason and approved by the stewards. The entry fee shall be refunded for scratches made in compliance with the above conditions. Starters to be named through the entry box at the usual time of closing. All supplementary nominations will be required to pay entry and starting fees if they participate. Trophy to winning owner. Closed Saturday, April 8, 2006 with 54 nominations.

Value of Race: $114,900 Winner $68,389; second $22,061; third $11,030; fourth $5,515; fifth $3,309; sixth $1,149; seventh $1,149; eighth $1,149; ninth $1,149. Mutuel Pool $1,055,714.00 Exacta Pool $751,398.00 Trifecta Pool $524,869.00 Superfecta Pool $177,183.00

Last Raced	Horse	M/Eqt.	A.	Wt	PP	St	¼	½	¾	Str	Fin	Jockey	Odds $1
7Apr06 ^{9}Kee^{1}	Magnificent Song	L b	3	116	8	2	$5^{2\frac{1}{2}}$	6^{1}	5^{hd}	$6^{\frac{1}{2}}$	$1^{\frac{1}{2}}$	Gomez G K	6.00
7Apr06 ^{5}Kee^{1}	Fiery Dancer	L	3	116	5	3	2^{hd}	$2^{\frac{1}{2}}$	$2^{1\frac{1}{2}}$	1^{1}	$2^{\frac{3}{4}}$	Castellano J J	9.20
23Apr06 ^{8}Kee^{2}	May Night		3	122	6	6	6^{hd}	$7^{2\frac{1}{2}}$	$7^{1\frac{1}{2}}$	5^{hd}	3no	Albarado R J	4.00
11Mar06 ^{2}SA^{6}	Kitty Hawk-GB	L	3	116	4	9	8^{7}	8^{5}	8^{9}	$7^{1\frac{1}{2}}$	4no	Leparoux J R	2.10
25Mar06 ^{8}GP^{3}	Southern Protocol	L	3	116	9	1	$4^{2\frac{1}{2}}$	$4^{\frac{1}{2}}$	$3^{\frac{1}{2}}$	3^{1}	5^{nk}	Bejarano R	10.20
8Apr06 ^{9}Kee^{6}	Performing Diva	L	3	116	1	7	3^{hd}	$3^{\frac{1}{2}}$	4^{1}	4^{hd}	$6^{\frac{1}{2}}$	Prado E S	8.50
15Apr06 ^{7}OP^{4}	Beau Dare	L	3	116	2	4	1^{2}	$1^{1\frac{1}{2}}$	1^{hd}	$2^{\frac{1}{2}}$	7^{2}	Guidry M	6.50
25Mar06 ^{10}OP^{6}	Best Mom	L	3	116	7	5	7^{5}	5^{hd}	$6^{\frac{1}{2}}$	8^{20}	8	McKee J	11.20
	Runaway Nell	b	3	116	3	8	9	9	9	9	—	Toups R	35.60

OFF AT 1:27 Start Good. Won driving. Course firm.

TIME $:23^4$, $:47^4$, $1:11^4$, $1:35^4$, 1:42 (:23.81, :47.91, 1:11.88, 1:35.97, 1:42.15)

$2 Mutuel Prices:

9 – MAGNIFICENT SONG	14.00	7.40	4.80
6 – FIERY DANCER		9.00	5.40
7 – MAY NIGHT			3.60

$2 EXACTA 9–6 PAID $101.00 $2 TRIFECTA 9–6–7 PAID $456.00
$2 SUPERFECTA 9–6–7–5 PAID $1,537.80

Gr/ro. f, (Apr), by Unbridled's Song – Song to Remember, by Storm Cat. Trainer Pletcher Todd A. Bred by ClassicStar (Ky).

SIXTH RACE
Churchill
MAY 5, 2006

1 1/16 MILES. (1.41^{1}) 3RD RUNNING OF THE ALYSHEBA. Purse $100,000 FOR THREE YEAR OLDS AND UPWARD. By subscription of $100 each on or before April 8, 2006 or by Supplementary Nomination of $5,000 at time of entry. $500 to pass the entry box; $500 additional to start, with $100,000 added. After payment of 1% to all owners of horses finishing sixth through last, 62% of the remaining purse shall be paid to the owner of the winner, 20% to second, 10% to third, 5% to fourth and 3% to fifth. Three-year-olds 117 lbs.; Older 124 lbs. Non-winners of $50,000 twice at a mile or over in 2006 allowed 2 lbs.; $50,000 at a mile or over in 2006, 4 lbs.; two races at a mile or over other than maiden or claiming in 2006, 6 lbs. Starters to be named through the entry box at the usual time of closing. All supplementary nominations will be required to pay entry and starting fees if they participate. Trophy to winning owner. Closed Saturday, April 8, 2006 with 55 nominations.

Value of Race: $114,500 Winner $68,861; second $22,214; third $11,106; fourth $5,553; fifth $3,331; sixth $1,145; seventh $1,145; eighth $1,145. Mutuel Pool $1,252,627.00 Exacta Pool $895,349.00 Trifecta Pool $647,488.00 Superfecta Pool $203,408.00

Last Raced	Horse	M/Eqt.	A.	Wt	PP	St	¼	½	¾	Str	Fin	Jockey	Odds $1
8Apr06 11OP3	Gouldings Green	L	5	118	4	3	4 hd	5 1½	3½	2 3	1 hd	Lanerie C J	1.50
17Jly05 9FE3	Wild Desert	L b	4	118	6	1	3 2	3 1	2 1	1 hd	2 4½	Bejarano R	1.90
8Apr06 11OP8	Andromeda's Hero	L	4	118	7	4	7 3	7 hd	8	3½	3 4¼	Gomez G K	6.40
7Jan06 10LaD6	M B Sea	L b	7	118	2	8	8	8	7½	4 2	4 2	Douglas R R	10.40
11Mar06 8Tam2	Seek Gold	L	6	118	8	7	6 3	6 4½	5 1½	5½	5 3	Melancon L	14.20
12Apr06 9OP3	Greater Good	L b	4	118	1	5	5 2½	4 hd	6 1	7 3	6 4¼	McKee J	9.30
19Apr06 2Kee1	Artemus Sunrise	L	5	118	3	2	1 hd	2½	4½	6 2	7 4½	Castanon J L	20.30
14Apr06 9Mnr4	Chippewa Trail	L b	5	118	5	6	2½	1 2½	1 hd	8	8	Leparoux J R	38.40

OFF AT 2:12 Start Good. Won driving. Track fast.

TIME :23^{3}, :46^{3}, 1:11^{2}, 1:36, 1:42^{1} (:23.75, :46.79, 1:11.59, 1:36.09, 1:42.37)

$2 Mutuel Prices:

6 – GOULDINGS GREEN	5.00	2.80	2.20
8 – WILD DESERT		4.00	3.00
9 – ANDROMEDA'S HERO			3.20

$2 EXACTA 6–8 PAID $20.20 $2 TRIFECTA 6–8–9 PAID $80.80
$2 SUPERFECTA 6–8–9–4 PAID $257.60

Ch. h, (Apr), by Charismatic – Elusive Gold , by Strike the Gold . Trainer Reinstedler Anthony. Bred by Marvin Delfiner (Ky).

SEVENTH RACE
Churchill
MAY 5, 2006

5 FURLONGS. (Turf) (.55^{2}) 12TH RUNNING OF THE AEGON TURF SPRINT. Grade III. Purse $100,000 FOR THREE-YEAR-OLDS AND UPWARD. By subscription of $100 each on or before April 8, 2006 or by Supplementary Nomination of $5,000 at time of entry. $500 to pass the entry box; $500 additional to start, with $100,000 added. After payment of 1% to the owners of the horses finishing sixth through last, 62% of the remaining purse shall be paid to the winner, 20% to second, 10% to third, 5% to fourth and 3% to fifth. Three-year-olds 118 lbs.; Older 124 lbs. Non-winners of $50,000 on the turf in 2006 allowed 2lbs.; a sweepstake on the turf in 2005–2006, 4 lbs.; $24,000 on the turf since July 4, 6 lbs.

Value of Race: $116,000 Winner $66,886; second $21,576; third $10,788; fourth $5,394; fifth $3,236; sixth $1,160; seventh $1,160; eighth $1,160; ninth $1,160; tenth $1,160; eleventh $1,160; twelfth $1,160. Mutuel Pool $1,308,657.00 Exacta Pool $929,645.00 Trifecta Pool $718,771.00 Superfecta Pool $255,720.00

Last Raced	Horse	M/Eqt.	A.	Wt	PP	St	3/16	3/8	Str	Fin	Jockey	Odds $1
14Apr06 7Kee3	Man Of Illusion-Aus	L	5	118	9	5	5 1½	4½	3 1½	1 nk	Leparoux J R	2.40
14Apr06 7Kee8	Justice for Auston	L	7	118	8	3	3 hd	3½	2 1½	2¾	Douglas R R	38.80
14Apr06 7Kee1	Atticus Kristy	L b	5	124	5	11	7½	7 1	4 hd	3 1	Gomez G K	3.70
14Apr06 7Kee9	Mighty Beau	L	7	122	12	7	6 hd	6 hd	5 1½	4 nk	Solis A	7.20
15Apr06 4GP2	Western Kind	b	5	122	3	2	1 hd	1 hd	1½	5½	Bejarano R	5.20
9Apr06 3SA4	Geronimo-Chi	L b	7	122	4	6	11 2	9 1	8½	6 1¾	Espinoza V	10.00
15Apr06 4GP1	The Nth Degree	L	5	122	1	4	4 1½	5 1	7 2	7 no	Prado E S	14.20
8Jan06 10Tam3	Rockhurst	L b	7	122	11	9	9 hd	10 1	10 2	8¾	Guidry M	28.60
14Apr06 7Kee5	Sgt. Bert	L	5	122	7	8	8 1½	8 3	9 hd	9 1½	Albarado R J	10.20
14Apr06 7Kee7	Parker Run	L b	5	118	10	12	10 2	12	12	10 nk	Castanon J L	30.60
2Mar06 10GP7	Social Probation	L f	4	118	6	10	12	11 1½	11½	11 2½	Borel C H	26.00
2Apr06 8GG1	Lion Andthe Lamb	L b	5	118	2	1	2 2	2 2	6 hd	12	Baze R A	28.30

OFF AT 3:07 Start Good For All But ROCKHURST. Won driving. Course firm.

TIME :21^{4}, :44^{3}, :56^{1} (:21.90, :44.75, :56.28)

$2 Mutuel Prices:

9 – MAN OF ILLUSION-AUS	6.80	4.80	3.40
8 – JUSTICE FOR AUSTON		30.80	12.80
5 – ATTICUS KRISTY			3.20

$2 EXACTA 9–8 PAID $275.20 $2 TRIFECTA 9–8–5 PAID $1,192.00
$2 SUPERFECTA 9–8–5–12 PAID $6,235.00

B. h, (Sep), by Encosta de Lago-Aus – Raunchy Ruler-Aus , by Rancho Ruler-Aus . Trainer Biancone Patrick L. Bred by D H K Investments Pty Ltd (Aus).

EIGHTH RACE

Churchill

MAY 5, 2006

1$\frac{1}{16}$ MILES. (1.41^1) 21ST RUNNING OF THE LOUISVILLE BREEDERS' CUP HANDICAP. Grade II. Purse $300,000 (includes $100,000 BC – Breeders' Cup) FOR FILLIES AND MARES THREE YEARS OLD AND UPWARD. By subscription of $300 each on or before April 8, 2006 or by Supplementary Nomination of $15,000 each by the closing of entries on Friday, April 28, 2006. $1,500 to pass the entry box; $1,500 additional to start, with $200,000 added and an additional $100,000 from the Breeders' Cup Fund for Cup Nominees only. After payment of 1% of the host association's added monies to all owners of horses finishing sixth through last, 62% of the remaining purse shall be paid to the owner of the winner, 20% to second, 10% to third, 5% to fourth and 3% to fifth. Breeders' Cup Fund monies also correspondingly divided providing a Breeders' Cup nominee has finished first through fifth. Any Breeders' Cup Fund monies not awarded will revert back to the Fund. Weights to be announced Saturday, April 29, 2006. Starters to be named through the entry box at the usual time of closing. Trophy to winning owner given by Breeders' Cup Ltd. Closed Saturday, April 8, 2006 with 30 nominations.

Value of Race: $271,000 Winner $140,127; second $65,202; third $32,601; fourth $16,300; fifth $9,780; sixth $2,330; seventh $2,330; eighth $2,330. Mutuel Pool $1,567,176.00 Exacta Pool $1,032,291.00 Trifecta Pool $776,645.00 Superfecta Pool $257,418.00

Last Raced	Horse	M/Eqt.	A.	Wt	PP	St	$\frac{1}{4}$	$\frac{1}{2}$	$\frac{3}{4}$	Str	Fin	Jockey	Odds $1
25Mar06 9GP1	OonaghMaccool–Ire	L	4	117	1	7	42$\frac{1}{2}$	4$\frac{1}{2}$	3$\frac{1}{2}$	13$\frac{1}{2}$	13$\frac{3}{4}$	Bejarano R	1.60
8Apr06 9OP3	La Reason	L	6	114	5	2	6$\frac{1}{2}$	6hd	62	2$\frac{1}{2}$	25	Castellano J J	7.00
1Apr06 10TP1	Gallant Secret	L	4	114	8	4	5$\frac{1}{2}$	72	5hd	41	31$\frac{1}{4}$	Leparoux J R	22.00
19Apr06 8Kee4	In the Gold	L	4	119	4	5	31$\frac{1}{2}$	31$\frac{1}{2}$	41	52	41	Nakatani C S	14.20
9Apr06 9OP1	Capeside Lady	L	5	118	2	1	1$\frac{1}{2}$	11$\frac{1}{2}$	1$\frac{1}{2}$	32	53$\frac{1}{2}$	Bridgmohan S X	6.20
19Apr06 8Kee2	Private Gift	L	4	117	6	3	2$\frac{1}{2}$	2$\frac{1}{2}$	2$\frac{1}{2}$	62$\frac{1}{2}$	61$\frac{1}{4}$	Albarado R J	20.80
25Mar06 9GP2	Sweet Symphony	L	4	119	7	6	8	8	8	74$\frac{1}{2}$	715	Velasquez C	3.30
7Apr06 2SA2	Leave Me Alone	L b	4	117	3	8	7hd	5$\frac{1}{2}$	7$\frac{1}{2}$	8	8	Gomez G K	4.60

OFF AT 3:56 Start Good For All But OONAGH MACCOOL (IRE), LEAVE ME ALONE. Won driving. Track fast.

TIME :24^1, :47^4, 1:12^2, 1:36^4, 1:42^4 (:24.25, :47.93, 1:12.57, 1:36.81, 1:42.96)

$2 Mutuel Prices:

1 – OONAGH MACCOOL–IRE............	5.20	3.60	2.80
5 – LA REASON......................		6.80	4.40
8 – GALLANT SECRET..................			5.80

$2 EXACTA 1–5 PAID $32.40 $2 TRIFECTA 1–5–8 PAID $309.20
$2 SUPERFECTA 1–5–8–4 PAID $3,211.40

Ch. f, (Mar), by Giant's Causeway – Alidiva–Ire , by Chief Singer . Trainer Pletcher Todd A. Bred by C H Wacker III (Ire).

NINTH RACE

Churchill

MAY 5, 2006

1$\frac{1}{16}$ MILES. (Turf) (1.40^3) 15TH RUNNING OF THE CROWN ROYAL AMERICAN TURF. Grade III. Purse $100,000 FOR THREE–YEAR–OLDS. By subscription of $100 each on or before April 8, 2006 or by Supplementary Nomination of $5,000 at time of entry. $500 to pass the entry box; $500 additional to start, with $100,000 added. After payment of 1% to the owners of the horses finishing sixth through last, 62% of the remaining purse shall be paid to the owner of the winner, 20% to second, 10% to third, 5% to fourth and 3% to fifth. Weight 122 lbs. Non–winners of a sweepstakes on the turf allowed 2 lbs.; three races other than maiden or claiming, 4 lbs.; two races other than maiden or claiming, 6 lbs.

Value of Race: $114,300 Winner $70,158; second $22,632; third $11,316; fourth $5,657; fifth $3,394; sixth $1,143. Mutuel Pool $1,334,577.00 Exacta Pool $737,729.00 Trifecta Pool $466,815.00 Superfecta Pool $127,661.00

Last Raced	Horse	M/Eqt.	A.	Wt	PP	St	$\frac{1}{4}$	$\frac{1}{2}$	$\frac{3}{4}$	Str	Fin	Jockey	Odds $1
29Oct05 4Bel8	Stream Cat	b	3	122	1	6	6	6	6	32$\frac{1}{2}$	1nk	Leparoux J R	4.10
8Apr06 7Tam2	Go Between	L	3	122	4	1	21	31$\frac{1}{2}$	33	11	22$\frac{3}{4}$	Prado E S	1.40
7Apr06 3GP1	Gaelic Storm	L	3	117	5	2	11$\frac{1}{2}$	2$\frac{1}{2}$	1hd	2$\frac{1}{2}$	33	Douglas R R	10.70
8Apr06 8Kee1	Giant Basil	L	3	119	6	5	3hd	52$\frac{1}{2}$	4$\frac{1}{2}$	41$\frac{1}{2}$	42	Nakatani C S	3.20
20Apr06 8Kee3	Tahoe Warrior	L	3	116	3	3	4hd	11	2hd	51	53$\frac{3}{4}$	Gomez G K	3.70
25Mar06 9TP6	Warrior Within	L	3	118	2	4	53$\frac{1}{2}$	4hd	51	6	6	Bejarano R	17.50

OFF AT 4:48 Start Good. Won driving. Course firm.

TIME :24^3, :48^4, 1:12^4, 1:36^1, 1:42^1 (:24.76, :48.84, 1:12.92, 1:36.36, 1:42.27)

$2 Mutuel Prices:

2 – STREAM CAT......................	10.20	4.20	3.80
5 – GO BETWEEN.....................		2.80	2.40
6 – GAELIC STORM...................			3.60

$2 EXACTA 2–5 PAID $26.60 $2 TRIFECTA 2–5–6 PAID $199.60
$2 SUPERFECTA 2–5–6–7 PAID $439.20

Dk. b or br. g, (Feb), by Black Minnaloushe – Water Course , by Irish River–Fr . Trainer Biancone Patrick L. Bred by Matthews Breeding and Racing Ltd (Ky).

TENTH RACE
Churchill
MAY 5, 2006

1⅛ MILES. (1.47^{1}) 132ND RUNNING OF THE KENTUCKY OAKS. Grade I. Purse $500,000 FILLIES, THREE YEARS OLD. By subscription of $100 each on or before February 11, 2006, or by Supplementary Nomination of $25,000 each at the time of entry. $2,500 to pass the entry box; $2,500 additonal to start, with $500,000 added. After payment of 1% to the owners of the horses finishing sixth through last, 62% of the remaining purse shall be paid to the owner of the winner, 20% to second, 10% to third, 5% to fourth and 3% to fifth. Weight 121 lbs.

Value of Race: $685,310 Winner $386,395; second $124,834; sixth $6,859; third $62,417; fourth $31,208; fifth $18,725; seventh $6,859; eighth $6,859; ninth $6,859; tenth $6,859; eleventh $6,859; twelfth $6,859; thirteenth $6,859; fourteenth $6,859. Mutuel Pool $3,589,571.00 Exacta Pool $2,115,196.00 Trifecta Pool $1,874,345.00 Superfecta Pool $707,482.00

Last Raced	Horse	M/Eqt.	A.	Wt	PP	St	¼	½	¾	Str	Fin	Jockey	Odds $1
25Mar06 ^{8}TP^{3}	Lemons Forever	L	3	121	14	12	14	14	10^{hd}	$5^{1\frac{1}{2}}$	$1^{1\frac{1}{2}}$	Guidry M	47.10
25Mar06 ^{10}OP^{1}	Ermine	L	3	121	12	6	$1^{1\frac{1}{2}}$	12^{1}	9^{2}	$3^{\frac{1}{2}}$	$2^{1\frac{1}{4}}$	Albarado R J	10.50
8Apr06 ^{9}Kee^{1}	[D]Bushfire	L	3	121	10	4	$4^{\frac{1}{2}}$	$4^{\frac{1}{2}}$	3^{1}	2^{1}	3^{1}	Velasquez C	5.80
8Apr06 ^{9}Kee^{2}	Wait a While	L	3	121	8	5	6^{2}	5^{hd}	$5^{\frac{1}{2}}$	4^{hd}	$4^{1\frac{1}{4}}$	Gomez G K	8.30
5Mar06 ^{8}GP^{2}	Wonder LadyAnneL	L	3	121	7	13	7^{hd}	8^{1}	$4^{\frac{1}{2}}$	6^{3}	$5^{\frac{1}{2}}$	Prado E S	8.20
15Apr06 ^{1}Kee^{1}	Red Cherries Spin	L f	3	121	5	3	$3^{1\frac{1}{2}}$	$3^{1\frac{1}{2}}$	1^{hd}	1^{hd}	$6^{1\frac{1}{4}}$	Nakatani C S	34.40
24Mar06 ^{8}Aqu^{1}	Last Romance	L	3	121	13	11	$12^{\frac{1}{2}}$	9^{hd}	12^{4}	9^{5}	7^{1}	Bejarano R	28.30
25Mar06 ^{8}TP^{1}	Top Notch Lady	L	3	121	11	10	13^{3}	11^{1}	$7^{\frac{1}{2}}$	8^{2}	8^{hd}	Husbands P	32.40
14Apr06 ^{10}OP^{6}	Quiet Kim	L	3	121	3	7	8^{hd}	7^{2}	8^{hd}	7^{hd}	9^{8}	Desormeaux K J	31.80
8Apr06 ^{9}Kee^{4}	Itty Bitty Pretty	L b	3	121	9	9	$10^{\frac{1}{2}}$	$13^{2\frac{1}{2}}$	13^{5}	$10^{\frac{1}{2}}$	10^{4}	Valenzuela P A	17.90
8Apr06 ^{9}Kee^{3}	Balance	L b	3	121	4	8	5^{hd}	6^{hd}	$6^{\frac{1}{2}}$	$11^{\frac{1}{2}}$	$11^{8\frac{1}{4}}$	Espinoza V	1.60
14Apr06 ^{10}OP^{2}	Miss Norman	L b	3	121	1	1	$1^{1\frac{1}{2}}$	$1^{2\frac{1}{2}}$	11^{2}	13^{12}	12no	Morales P	23.00
13Apr06 ^{8}Kee^{1}	Diplomat Lady	L	3	121	2	2	2^{2}	$2^{1\frac{1}{2}}$	$2^{\frac{1}{2}}$	12^{6}	13	Solis A	10.20
14Apr06 ^{10}OP^{4}	Ex Caelis	L	3	121	6	14	9^{2}	10^{hd}	14	14	—	Leparoux J R	26.10

[D] – Bushfire disqualified and placed 6th

OFF AT 5:50 Start Good. Won driving. Track fast.

TIME :22^{2}, :46^{2}, 1:11^{2}, 1:37, 1:50 (:22.46, :46.45, 1:11.47, 1:37.14, 1:50.07)

$2 Mutuel Prices:

14 – LEMONS FOREVER	96.20	37.00	18.00
12 – ERMINE		11.20	7.80
8 – WAIT A WHILE			6.40

$2 EXACTA 14–12 PAID $985.60 $2 TRIFECTA 14–12–8 PAID $12,186.60
$2 SUPERFECTA 14–12–8–7 PAID $89,103.00

Ch. f, (May), by Lemon Drop Kid – Critikola-Arg , by Tough Critic . Trainer Stewart Dallas. Bred by Farfellow Farms Ltd (Ky).

ELEVENTH RACE
Churchill
MAY 5, 2006

6 FURLONGS. (1.07^{2}) MAIDEN SPECIAL WEIGHT . Purse $50,000 (includes $10,000 KTDF - Kentucky TB Devt Fund) FOR MAIDENS, FILLIES AND MARES THREE YEARS OLD AND UPWARD. Three Year Olds, 118 lbs.; Older, 124 lbs. (Preference to horses that have not started for $30,000 or less in last 5 starts).

Value of Race: $49,500 Winner $31,300; second $10,000; third $5,000; fourth $2,000; fifth $1,200. Mutuel Pool $876,442.00 Exacta Pool $578,498.00 Trifecta Pool $501,772.00 Superfecta Pool $197,072.00

Last Raced	Horse	M/Eqt.	A.	Wt	PP	St	¼	½	Str	Fin	Jockey	Odds $1
5Feb06 ^{3}SA^{6}	Touch Me Once	L b	3	113	8	6	6^{hd}	5^{3}	3^{hd}	$1^{\frac{3}{4}}$	Leparoux J R^{5}	4.40
	Arradoul	L	3	118	10	1	$2^{\frac{1}{2}}$	$1^{1\frac{1}{2}}$	1^{1}	$2^{\frac{3}{4}}$	Lanerie C J	3.10
25Mar06 ^{2}TP^{4}	Privy's Jewel	L	3	118	7	7	8^{4}	$4^{\frac{1}{2}}$	$2^{1\frac{1}{2}}$	$3^{1\frac{1}{2}}$	Bejarano R	2.50
	Keltish Lass	L	3	118	5	5	9^{1}	9^{4}	$5^{2\frac{1}{2}}$	$4^{2\frac{1}{4}}$	Guidry M	12.90
26Feb06 ^{9}GP^{5}	Celestial Princess	L	3	118	3	3	$4^{1\frac{1}{2}}$	2^{hd}	4^{3}	$5^{5\frac{1}{2}}$	Velasquez C	3.20
	High Priestess	L	3	111	2	9	$3^{\frac{1}{2}}$	7^{1}	7^{4}	$6^{4\frac{3}{4}}$	Toups R^{7}	40.50
25Mar06 ^{6}TP^{8}	Fly to the Stars	L	3	118	1	10	10	10	8^{2}	7^{hd}	Hernandez B J Jr	40.70
26Dec05 ^{6}TP^{11}	Golden Say	L	3	118	4	4	$5^{\frac{1}{2}}$	3^{2}	$6^{\frac{1}{2}}$	$8^{5\frac{1}{2}}$	Johnson J M	29.50
	Fat Tale	L b	3	118	9	8	7^{1}	6^{1}	9^{6}	$9^{8\frac{3}{4}}$	Butler D P	13.00
23Apr06 ^{5}Kee^{9}	Angelina P.	L	3	118	6	2	$1^{\frac{1}{2}}$	$8^{\frac{1}{2}}$	10	10	Teator P A	36.90

OFF AT 6:29 Start Good. Won driving. Track fast.

TIME :21^{4}, :45^{4}, :58^{1}, 1:11 (:21.86, :45.87, :58.37, 1:11.10)

$2 Mutuel Prices:

8 – TOUCH ME ONCE	10.80	5.20	3.40
10 – ARRADOUL		5.00	3.40
7 – PRIVY'S JEWEL			2.80

$2 EXACTA 8–10 PAID $48.20 $2 TRIFECTA 8–10–7 PAID $166.20
$2 SUPERFECTA 8–10–7–5 PAID $951.60

Ch. f, (May), by Touch Gold – Theresa the Teacha , by Cure the Blues . Trainer Dollase Wallace. Bred by John Gunther & Fred Sahadi (Ky).

Most of the handicapping angles and factors that were discussed in the earlier chapters can be successfully implemented for both Oaks Day and Derby Day, and are sure to leave you well ahead of the general racing public. Veteran New York handicapper Dave Litfin addressed this topic in his newly released and updated *Expert Handicapping: Winning Insights into Betting Thoroughbreds* (DRF Press 2007) when he wrote, "But beyond all the color and pageantry of big-race days, their real appeal to serious players is undoubtedly the fact that they offer prime opportunities to capitalize on exceptional value situations. The crowds are large, everyone's there to have a good time, and the payoffs for logical sequences of results are usually astounding."

Nevertheless, the pitfalls associated with wagering on the Kentucky Derby and the Oaks are unique in all of Thoroughbred racing. There is frequently a large and competitive field of still-developing 3-year-olds and many are running on an unfamiliar surface, in unfamiliar surroundings. Numerous 3-year-olds that have had great success at the middle distances have struggled enormously at the $1\frac{1}{4}$-mile classic distance of the Derby. Many a bettor who has attempted to uncover Derby winners using traditional handicapping methods has failed miserably and watched his or her selection run up the track.

BEYER PAR FOR THE OAKS

IF YOU CAN'T recall what we discussed back in Chapter 2 when we first reviewed Beyer Speed Figures, here's a refresher course. A Beyer par is the average winning Beyer number for a particular class level. In the case of the Kentucky Oaks, we can look at the Beyer Speed Figure earned by previous winners and retrieve an average number, or par, that is usually required to win the race, just as we did with the Derby. The par is helpful in that we can study the past performances for the current year's Oaks contenders and get a sense for which fillies might have already achieved the Oaks par, or better yet, which ones might be progressing enough to run a number that will win the race.

Our sample starts in 1992 with Luv Me Luv Me Not and runs through last year's winner, Rags to Riches. *Daily Racing Form* started printing Beyer Speed Figures in 1992, which gives us an adequate 16-year sample. Following is the list of Oaks winners and their respective Beyer numbers.

Oaks Winner	Year	Beyer Speed Figure
Rags to Riches	(2007)	104
Lemons Forever	(2006)	92
Summerly	(2005)	90
Ashado	(2004)	102
Bird Town	(2003)	101
Farda Amiga	(2002)	103
Flute	(2001)	99
Secret Status	(2000)	100
Silverbulletday	(1999)	107
Keeper Hill	(1998)	100
Blushing K. D.	(1997)	104
Pike Place Dancer	(1996)	101
Gal in a Ruckus	(1995)	99
Sardula	(1994)	99
Dispute	(1993)	93
Luv Me Luv Me Not	(1992)	90

Average Winning Oaks Beyer: **99**

Now that we know the Beyer par for the Kentucky Oaks is 99, let's examine the Beyer figures these fillies earned in their last few starts before the Oaks. As we did when evaluating the Derby, we can uncover some clues or patterns for potential winners and expose solid candidates based on the numbers they have run in their prep races. Listed below are each Oaks winner's last three Beyer Speed Figures prior to the race. Can you recognize any patterns on your own? What Oaks winners had already reached par even before the race?

*Each Beyer Speed Figure that reached or exceeded 100 is indicated in bold.

	Prior to Oaks	Two Back	Three Back
Rags to Riches (2007)	96	93	88
Lemons Forever (2006)	76	86	78
Summerly (2005)	68	95	96
Ashado (2004)	97	94	84
Bird Town (2003)	98	**100**	84
Farda Amiga (2002)	95	84	70
Flute (2001)	99	85	90

	Prior to Oaks	Two Back	Three Back
Secret Status (2000)	82	92	91
Silverbulletday (1999)	**108**	**101**	**100**
Keeper Hill (1998)	89	95	75
Blushing K. D. (1997)	**110**	**102**	**103**
Pike Place Dancer (1996)	91	96	96
Gal in a Ruckus (1995)	84	75	84
Sardula (1994)	**104**	98	95
Dispute (1993)	95	94	83
Luv Me Luv Me Not (1992)	91	84	79

Out of the 16 Oaks winners and 48 total prep races calculated prior to each filly's Kentucky Oaks, *only* 19 percent of the winners reached or exceeded a 99 Beyer Speed Figure before the race. What this proves is that many Oaks winners blossom by posting a new Beyer top in the Oaks itself. This is extremely important handicapping data that can be used in your favor on Oaks Day. As the following list indicates, there have been nine fillies in the last 16 editions (56 percent) who earned their Beyer top on Oaks Day. There would have been 10 if we counted Flute, who posted a 99 Beyer in the Grade 1 Santa Anita Oaks nearly two months before equaling that figure in the Oaks.

	Oaks Beyer	Prior to Oaks	Two Back	Three Back
Rags to Riches	**104**	96	93	88
Lemons Forever	**92**	76	86	78
Ashado	**102**	97	94	84
Bird Town	**101**	98	**100**	84
Farda Amiga	**103**	95	84	70
Secret Status	**100**	82	92	91
Keeper Hill	**100**	89	95	75
Pike Place Dancer	**101**	91	96	96
Gail in a Ruckus	**99**	84	75	84

POST POSITION FOR THE OAKS

WHEN WE DISCUSSED acquiring some helpful handicapping data from a review of previous Kentucky Derby post-position results, we stressed the importance of not only tracking the winning outcome, but also looking at the other horses that filled out the underneath exotics. For those interested in wagering on intra-race exotic bets, these results were just as valuable as tracking the winning data. The same can be said for tracking the post positions for the Kentucky Oaks. The following are results from the 1995 running through the 2007 winner, Rags to Riches.

Post	Starts	Win	Place	Show	4th	Win %	ITM %	Super ITM %
1	13	1	1	0	3	7%	15%	38%
2	13	1	1	1	0	7%	23%	23%
3	13	1	1	3	3	7%	38%	61%
4	**13**	**5**	**2**	**1**	**1**	**38%**	**61%**	**69%**
5	13	2	0	3	1	15%	38%	46%
6	13	0	2	2	1	0%	30%	38%
7	12	0	0	1	2	0%	8%	25%
8	10	0	2	0	1	0%	20%	30%
9	8	1	1	0	0	12%	25%	25%
10	7	0	0	1	0	0%	14%	14%
11	7	1	2	1	0	14%	57%	57%
12	6	0	1	0	1	0%	16%	33%
13	5	0	0	0	0	0%	0%	0%
14	3	1	0	0	0	33%	0%	0%

*The Kentucky Oaks is limited to 14 starting positions.

A quick analysis uncovers that post 4 has been the most productive in the Oaks with 38 percent winners and 61 percent in-the-money finishes, and it has rounded out the superfecta at nearly 70 percent. Some other interesting post-position facts: Posts 6, 7, and 8 are a combined 0 for 35, and post positions 1 through 5 have won 10 of the last 13 runnings.

SUNSHINE STATES = OAKS VICTORY

IN CHAPTER 6 we looked at the major preps leading up to the Kentucky Derby and found that Derby winners do not seem to emerge from any one specific part of the country. The path to the Kentucky Oaks is much more defined and usually begins in Florida or Southern California. In fact, 13 of the last 20 winners (65 percent) have started their 3-year-old campaigns from one of these two locales. This is an extremely valuable stat and an excellent place to start sifting out the next potential winner. The list below shows the last and next-to-last prep races for the previous 20 Kentucky Oaks winners.

Year	Winner	Last Prep Race	Next-to-Last Prep Race
2007	Rags to Riches	G1 Santa Anita Oaks (Ca.)	G1 Los Virgenes (Ca.)
2006	Lemons Forever	G3 Bourbonette (Ky.)	Optional Clm/NW1 (Ark.)
2005	Summerly	G1 Ashland (Ky.)	G2 Fair Grounds Oaks (La.)
2004	Ashado	G1 Ashland (Ky.)	G2 Fair Grounds Oaks (La.)
2003	Bird Town	G2 Beaumont (Ky.)	Charon Stakes (Fl.)
2002	Farda Amiga	G1 Santa Anita Oaks (Ca.)	Optional Clm/NW1 (Ca.)
2001	Flute	G1 Santa Anita Oaks (Ca.)	Maiden Special Weight (Ca.)
2000	Secret Status	G3 Florida Oaks (Fl.)	G2 Davona Dale (Fl.)
1999	Silverbulletday	G1 Ashland (Ky.)	G3 Fair Grounds Oaks (La.)
1998	Keeper Hill	G1 Santa Anita Oaks (Ca.)	G1 Los Virgenes (Ca.)
1997	Blushing K. D.	G2 Fantasy (Ark.)	G3 Fair Grounds Oaks (La.)
1996	Pike Place Dancer	G3 Cal Derby (Ca.)	San Jose Stakes (Ca.)
1995	Gal in a Ruckus	Allowance (Ky.)	G3 Golden Rod (Ky.)
1994	Sardula	Santa Paula (Ca.)	G1 H'wd. Starlet (Ca.)
1993	Dispute	G2 Bonnie Miss (Fl.)	Allowance Race (Fl.)
1992	Luv Me Luv Me Not	G2 Arkansas Derby (Ark.)	G2 Jim Beam (Ky.)

1991	Lite Light	G2 Fantasy (Ark.)	G1 Santa Anita Oaks (Ca.)
1990	Seaside Attraction	G3 Beaumont (Ky.)	Allowance Race (Ca.)
1989	Open Mind	Pimlico Oaks (Md.)	G2 Bonnie Miss (Fl.)
1988	Goodbye Halo	G1 Santa Anita Oaks (Ca.)	G1 Las Virgenes (Ca.)

OAKS LEADING TRAINERS AND JOCKEYS

THE LATE Hall of Fame trainer Woody Stephens holds the Kentucky Oaks record with five winners: Hidden Talent, 1959; Make Sail, 1960; Sally Ship, 1963; White Star Line, 1978; and Heavenly Cause, 1981. Jockeys Eddie Arcaro and Manuel Ycaza are tied with the most wins at four.

An up-to-date idea of the success and failures of recent jockeys and trainers can be gleaned from looking at the past couple of decades. The following jockeys and trainers are singled out here because they have either had multiple Oaks wins in the last two decades, have had multiple wins or success in the race over a larger portion of time, or have yet to find the winner's circle despite several attempts.

Trainer D. Wayne Lukas (4 victories)
1990 Seaside Attraction (Chris McCarron)
1989 Open Mind (Angel Cordero Jr.)
1984 Lucky Lucky Lucky (Angel Cordero Jr.)
1982 Blush With Pride (William Shoemaker)

Trainer Jerry Hollendorfer (2 victories)
1996 Pike Place Dancer (Corey Nakatani)
1991 Lite Light (Corey Nakatani)

Trainer Bobby Frankel (2 victories)
2001 Flute (Jerry Bailey)
1998 Keeper Hill (David Flores)

Trainer Todd Pletcher (2 victories)
2007 Rags to Riches (Garrett Gomez)
2004 Ashado (John Velazquez)

Jockey Jerry Bailey (3 victories)
2005 Summerly
2001 Flute
1993 Dispute

The Oaks Goose-Egg Club
(*The following jockeys listed are still active)
Jockey Alex Solis (0 for 8)
Jockey Kent Desormeaux (0 for 8)

About the Author

DEAN KEPPLER is the director of DRF Press for *Daily Racing Form*. He has more than 25 years of experience handicapping both Thoroughbred and harness racing. Keppler was the 2005 winner of the Freehold Raceway Thoroughbred handicapping contest, and was the proud owner of a $91,000 pick-six ticket at Santa Anita Park on Easter Sunday, 2006. He has authored several books, including *Trainer Angles: Maximizing Profits Using Formulator Software and Advanced Trainer Stats*. He resides in Yonkers, New York, five minutes from the historic Yonkers Raceway now known as the new and improved Empire City.